A BUNCH OF THOUGHTS

About Notion Press

Notion Press is a Self-Publishing platform to write, publish & sell Print books and eBooks around the world. To learn more, visit www.notionpress.com

A BUNCH OF THOUGHTS is a product of the Notion Press Author Incubation Program.

A BUNCH OF THOUGHTS

V V RAMPAL

notionpress.com

Notion Press

5 Muthu Kalathy Street, Triplicane, Chennai - 600005

First Published by Notion Press

ISBN: 9789383185818

CONTENTS

PREFACE

I have placed a few thoughts for readers to share with me. They may not be thematically consistent but they show a thinking that comes to mind from time to time and from day to day. One may find the thoughts heavily loaded in favor of spiritual thinking but that is because I have thought of this subject for the last fifteen years and expressed myself in this vein in the last four books that I wrote. This is my fifth attempt to share my thinking with people through the published word.

In spiritual writing when we talk of God we tend to put a gender to that noun. But this does not mean we assign a specific gender to God since God is a universal presence and not a specific being. Assigning a gender is only a convenience of expression and nothing more. In addition, attaching a masculine gender elsewhere is no indication that we are partial to the male gender. It could easily be the other gender. The same applies to whenever we express the third person singular. I have no desire to be male oriented when I write he or him rather than she or her in the text. It is only a traditional way of expression which some have changed while others like me have not. One should therefore not feel offended by such expression of pronoun in the text..

This book is composed of thoughts that include spiritual values, reminiscences, opinions and expressions on topics that essentially concern spiritual growth and practice of ethical values. They may not constitute a coherent line of thought on one topic since they are written as they came. It is an exercise in thinking rather than a particular view presented on a specific topic. It is more like recording a thought a day. I have enjoyed writing them and hope they will interest the reader as well.

I welcome any opinion contrary to mine and would feel thankful if any suggestions come from the readers.

I thankfully acknowledge the interesting interaction with my friend Shri Surendra Pal who read the script and offered useful suggestions.

SEEKING THE INFINITE AND ETERNAL

OPTING FOR A SPIRITUAL WAY OF LIFE

It was an exhilarating experience. The soft breeze from the lakeside refreshed me and made me feel grateful to the creator for providing such a pleasing environment. The calm water of the lake and the serene environment of the setting sun was enough to soothe any frayed nerves. In this atmosphere of rustling trees and cool rippling water, no one could remain agitated. Serenity prevailed all around and one felt the caress of nature as if one was in the lap of mother. No wonder, nature is compared to mother. It makes you forget all worries and be assured of the comfort, caring and the soothing touch that one associates with the mother.

I was enjoying this cool confidence of being one with nature when a person passed me by. Completely ignoring me, he went ahead and sat on the grassy patch that extended up to the lake. Soon, he took the lotus pose and went in meditation.

Instinctively I felt like talking to him but looking to his meditative posture I decided otherwise. He was in deep concentration and it is indeed a sin to disturb a person in meditation. After about an hour or so, he came back to this world and started to rise. I quickly went to him and asked, ' sir, I am impressed to see you meditating with such concentration and am curious to know what you gain from all this. I think it is more enjoyable to feel the cool breeze and take in the beautiful scenery all around. But you shut your eyes and ears to all this.'

In reply to my comment he simply smiled and said, 'you would know the difference if you were in my position. Enjoyment of senses is temporary. I want something that is more permanent and elevating.'

This made me more inquisitive and I asked, 'what makes you think that there is something more enjoyable than the pleasure of the senses?' This query made him serious and he said, 'I do not know if you are ready to understand the implication of your statement, for there is a difference between enjoyment pf pleasure and feeling the bliss of existence. You must have the urge to move up in consciousness to appreciate the difference between sense pleasure and meditative bliss. Not all people are satisfied with their state of existence. They want to know the purpose of existence and wish to become a better and more enlightened person than their sensuous existence enables them to be. They are prepared to face struggle in life to know more about self and who they are. They want to know why they are here and what is the relevance of their life to this creation. They are curious about the possibility of other states of consciousness that seers have talked about and want to experience those states. Like any other struggle in life, the answers to these questions require an effort of high order. I am only a student who is trying to learn the secrets of life. I am not content with what I have. I want to know if there is more to this life. I want to raise the level of my understanding so as to know if the divine life exists. In my view, life is a continuous process of learning.

The moment you stop learning, you no longer need to live.'

Knowing that he was in a mood to talk, I encouraged him by asking, 'do you believe that our consciousness has other states which are more enlightened than the present one?' He jumped on this bait and said, 'that is what I am trying to experience. It is believed that the infinite consciousness expresses itself in nature through us and it is our duty to search for and develop our divine nature through spiritual practices. This is the eternal quest of man. The experience of higher states of consciousness is the purpose of spiritual life. It is a meeting of the human with the divine. There are persons, though only a few, who want to achieve this in their lifetime as the ultimate purpose of life. They are not satisfied with the limited nature of sense-based existence. They want to go beyond sense experience and achieve unity with the Infinite and Eternal. Like any other journey of experiences, this too has its problems. But the inquisitive and the brave always like to venture into the unknown. There lies the adventure of life. There is a ceaseless urge in them to experiment and learn more. That is what I am trying to do in my own humble way. It is not important to what degree I succeed. What is important is to go on trying.'

Needless to say, I was quite impressed by his sincerity and wished him well. There are indeed people who know what they want from their life, though there are many who waste it on frivolous activities and transitory enjoyments.

I came to the world thinking I would enjoy the life
But God smiled and said, 'you fool, you have been sent
To know thyself, and to experience the reality of existence;
I will not give you another chance in a million years,
So make the most of it and learn the lesson of life.'

Living in a garden, I loved the flowers
Not knowing that flower bushes have thorns too.

When humans talk of love, they mean it for a specific being
When God speaks of love, He means it for one and all.

Do not waste time in rituals and rites
To appease gods for your gain
Instead, rise in knowledge and devotion
And acknowledge the fact that a perfect human is truly divine.

I had known that day follows night
But when I opened my eyes from slumber,
I found darkness all around.
I closed my eyes and ears
And looked within
A cold light was shining
And spreading brightness all around

THE REST-HOUSE KEEPER

'We have to get down at the next station, so start packing.'

'Don't worry. I am almost ready for I have very little to pack'

Soon we were on the small platform that was almost deserted except for one or two railway staff to attend to their duties. When we came out of the station, it was the time when shadows lengthen by the minute and every one returns to home, weary and tired, for getting respite from the hard work necessary to make a living. After some wait and search, we got the transport to take us to our resting place.

The rest house was in a forest that had become dark with the shadows of tall trees One needed some courage to enter that old, dark, and lonely place that looked more like a haunted ruin of past century. We were met at the gate by a middle-aged man who welcomed us with a smile and took our bags to the rooms that we had booked. He told us that he was the keeper cum watchman cum cook and that we should not expect any other person to be present at that place since no body wanted to remain there for more than a day. We could easily see the truth in his statement because the haunting environment was enough to frighten any body that came to reside there. The silence of the place added to the eerie atmosphere that only the brave could venture to enjoy..

After an early supper, we decided to go to bed. But soon I realized that sleep was eluding me. The sound of nocturnal creatures and hoots of owl was the only sound that disturbed the stillness of forest at night. I thought of taking a walk and searched the premises for any book that I could use to induce sleep. To my surprise I found a room full of books that presumably was used as a library of sort. I found to my greater surprise the keeper browsing through a book. It was indeed something that I had not visualized even in my wildest dreams. I had thought that the man had his hands full with work since he was single-handedly managing the rest house. To find time for reading was highly unexpected from him in his position. I therefore went to him and asked, 'how is it that with all the work here you manage to find time for reading? Have you been living here long? How come there is no other person here except you?' I felt myself shooting questions without any reason or warning to the keeper and it made me a little embarrassed though my curiosity took better of me. The keeper too was surprised to face suddenly a barrage of questions, which he did not expect. However, he took his eyes off from the book and gently answered, 'you are right that I am the only person around in this place. The reason is that no body likes to stay here for long. As to my finding time for books, I like to read and when there is will there is always a way. Regarding my presence in this job, I must go back a few years in time when I was working as a medical assistant in the village dispensary. I used to enjoy my work since it involved helping people in relieving their physical suffering. But I had a streak of protest whenever somebody tried to do wrong and deceive people. As a consequence of this trait, I earned the wrath of many persons in the village and became an undesirable being. This news went to the notice of the village head and I lost my job. I thought with my qualification I would soon get another job in some other village. But the news about my strange habit of taking up cudgels on behalf of others prevented me to succeed. I was indeed feeling quite dejected when one day the keeper of this place happened to come to our village to pick up a helping hand. I talked to him and he agreed to take me even though this job was quite below my qualifications and experience. This is how I came here. As to me being alone, after I came here, the keeper left after some time and the whole responsibility of the place fell on me. But I don't regret. The place suits my temperament. I like solitude and scenic environment. I can still serve people and find time to read. The books are my friends here. Their company does not make any demands on me.'

With this he stopped and went back to his book. But he had aroused my curiosity about him. I therefore wanted to continue the talk and asked him, 'do you believe in destiny and God's purpose in creating us to live, learn and suffer for achieving higher goals?' On hearing this, he closed the book, placed it on the shelf and came nearer me and said,' yes, I believe in God but I am not a religious person in the conventional sense. I do not perform any rituals and my definition of God is not the same, as most people believe in. I consider him as only a supreme power that runs the universe with inviolable rules that we characterize as guiding principles. When I say him I do not mean him as a person but as a conscious energy devoid of any shape or form. I think that conscious energy is within us all and every living being is his form. Therefore you are as much a part of God as I am. In serving you I am serving God. That makes my job a truly noble one.

Regarding the destiny, I believe it is something that we make by our own actions. If I do your work satisfactorily, I make good destiny. It is the accumulated result of one's actions that results in one's so called destiny. If I make you angry I will receive your anger and that will be a bad destiny for me. I believe we are all created to undergo some experiences that make us wise in the long run. That I think is the purpose of God. In other words, the conscious energy expresses itself through us and we erroneously think that we are great individuals. Merging with God is like a part of energy joining the great ocean of creative energy. We become different shapes and sizes like the indestructible energy assuming different types of energy packs. To call one as being better than the other is sheer ignorance. We are all of the same stuff but of different thought patterns. The experiences of life are meant to change our thought patterns for the good of all. This is the lesson of life.

I hope you agree with me because you seem to be better educated than I am. I feel it is our excessive desires that separate us. You may have higher desires than I have. This makes you go for achieving higher status in society than I do. But at the core lies the same conscious energy, which expresses in you and me. You may feel slighted with this comparison, but since you asked I have said so. I hope you take it in the right spirit.

Any way, it is now getting late and I have to rise early in the morning to serve you the bed tea. I shall therefore end by saying there is nothing better that gives peace and joy than the feeling of equality and brotherhood. So let us go to our places with the feeling that tomorrow is another day.'

I must admit that I was completely floored by that keeper who went much beyond my expectations. I went to sleep with admiration and gratitude. No wonder this world is full of surprises.

THE PRIEST

'What do you do for a living' I asked the person who was sitting on the seat next to me. The bus was full to its capacity and the monotony of the journey was weighing heavily on me. It was important to start conversation in order to divert attention from the stuffy atmosphere in the crowded bus. Perhaps he too was anxious to talk because he soon replied, 'I work as a priest at a temple in Haridwar. I had gone to my place in the village for family reasons and am now returning to my work place.' He looked every inch a religious person. He had the vermilion mark on his forehead and wore the clothes that we normally associate with Hindu priests.

To continue the talk, I asked him why was so much importance given in scriptures on the need to improve the personal and social conduct in the spiritual journey when any body could go for worship and meditation without spending time on conduct improvement. This put him to thinking and after some time, he replied, 'can you make a pond without digging the earth? Do you boil the milk in a vessel without first cleaning it of dirt and oil? If you do so you are bound to spoil the milk. The same applies to your spiritual effort. You have to clean yourself in body, mind and intellect before divine spiritual energy can enter your being. You have to make yourself ready to receive the grace. When you completely clean yourself in body, mind and intellect, the divinity automatically flows into you.'

'OK.. That may be so, but what do you mean by cleaning in body, mind and intellect? Thoughts flow all the time and it is not possible to control them even if you wish to do so. Your mental make-up is a factor of so many parameters, some in your control and some out of your control. I know spiritual practice needs a discipline of high order but controlling thoughts is a different matter.'

The priest at this time became assertive and said, 'that is where it requires real effort. Cleaning the physical body is easy but cleaning the mind and intellect requires both time and effort of great magnitude. It is done primarily by applying yourself whole heartedly to the process of purifying the mind and intellect through the practice of truthfulness, honesty, love and compassion for all and restricting your desire to enjoy the pleasures of the senses. Contentment, austerity, penance, study of scriptures and repeating the name of God are helpful in achieving mental purity. Meditation keeps your mind away from polluting influences and makes you ready to receive the spiritual energy. The Divine enters only if the house is in order. It shies away from a cluttered mind and intellect. The cobwebs of negative thoughts have to be wiped clean. Unless you make your psychophysical apparatus suitable for receiving the desired energy, you cannot hope to succeed in your spiritual goal. Your mind needs to be tuned to the divine frequency similar to the tuning of a radio receiver. Without proper tuning you cannot receive the desired station.'

'I think I get your point,' I said to assure him. He had made a point that agreed with the practice of most religions. The emphasis on ethical and moral life is common in most religions. This is like cleaning the temple before installation of deity.

WHY DO I WORSHIP HIM?

Do I have to sing praises of Him?
When I know He is All-Merciful

Do I have to dance before Him?
When I know He is omniscient and knows my actions

Do I have to seek Him in temples?
When I know He is omnipresent

Do I have to recite His names loudly?
When I know He is the celestial sound Himself

Do I need to show him the light?
When I know He is light Himself

Do I need to worship Him with flowers and sweets?
When I know He is the creator of everything

Do I have to wake Him up and put to sleep?
When I know He made the day and night

Do I need to pray to Him?
When I know He gives me every thing I deserve without asking

Do I have to give charity in His name?
When I know He is the provider for all

Do I have to educate others about Him?

When I know He is pure consciousness incarnate

Do I need to prove His existence?
When I know He is Absolute Existence

Do I have to extol His powers?
When I know He is omnipotent

Do I have to limit Him in finite form?
When I know He is infinite and eternal

But I do all this
Because these activities are symbolic of my love for Him

THE REAL PURPOSE

He was a gentle and kind person who stood straight and smooth to a height of 6 feet. A faint smile was always present on his face. But he was a restless person. Always shifting places and jobs, one never knew when and where he moved at any given time. To most people who knew him, he was an elusive but a warm person. He talked in low tones, respectfully to his seniors in age and lovingly to younger ones. He had a loveable personality, jovial at times and sensible to the core. But he was not very sentimental. He looked to the world as a playground in which people played their game; some honestly, others deceptive and unkindly. Whenever any one picked up a quarrel with him, he soon disarmed him with his soft smile and kind words. I particularly liked him for his views on the approach to life and his curious nature.

One day I met him in a park when I was on an evening walk. He was engrossed in his thoughts when I confronted him and said,' how come you are so sad and serious today. This is quite unlike you. Is there something bothering you?' He asked me to sit down, for he wanted to talk to me. After a while, he said,' what do you think about the purpose of life? I have dissatisfaction about the role I am playing in this life. Can you tell me why do we come to this world? Is it to simply earn money and enjoy the pleasure of senses? Or is it to attain a status and position of strength to rule over others? It looks so meaningless to me that I wonder why this world was created if at all it was created for a purpose? I do not subscribe to the belief that the creation is a work of personalized God. If the creation is without purpose, what purpose can we mortals serve? Is it all an accident of nature? It is quite upsetting to see people being born, suffering and enjoying temporarily and then dying like insects. What good does that do to the creator, if at all there is a creator?'

It was a challenging question, which most people ask but find no satisfactory answer. Perhaps there is no valid answer in human literature though many attempts have been made to answer it. At least in science and logic there is no attempt to answer it. Only in religion and philosophy people have tried to talk of it and provided their views, which take one to imaginative world of hypotheses and assertions based on intuitive thought. I therefore kept quiet for a while and then said,' no answer can satisfy you unless you find yourself with you own experience. I can only say that in religious philosophy, they say that the aim of human existence is to know oneself. The aim of our existence is to know and experience that one is a spirit and not the body mind complex that we know ourselves to be. This is the spiritual aim that most religious people believe in, at least in Vedanta.

In some other religions too, they say, 'know thyself,' which amounts to the same concept of introspection and experience of spiritual nature of mankind. For a genuine seeker of truth however, it is necessary to try the spiritual path, and experience the self, in order to satisfy the curiosity. Merely believing the scriptural statements will not suffice. '

This interaction quieted him further and finally he said, 'yes, I think you have a point, but it needs verification'. After that we parted because it was becoming chilly.

I did not come across him for the next ten years or so. I had almost forgotten about him till one day I saw him in a gathering of sadhus that had come to a religious function where I also had gone. It was a pleasant surprise to see him in such a garb. I immediately went to him and greeted. He too seemed pleased to see me and asked, 'how are you? It is nice to see you again after a long gap.' I too said that it was indeed a happy coincidence to see him in such circumstances. But I could not contain my surprise to find him in sadhu's dress. I therefore asked him whether he had taken sanyas, to which he replied,

'I would not call it sanyas because that requires a great discipline of mind and body which I find difficult to sustain. But I am definitely in spiritual mood to understand the spiritual aspect of life.'

'But last time I met you, you did not show any inkling of this change though you did seem to be rather unsatisfied with your then prosperous life.' I said this to remind him of our last meeting.

'Yes I remember our last meeting where I had said that the spiritual path needs to be verified before I accept it. You then had presented three aims of life, which I thought of experiencing myself in order to see which one fulfills the right purpose.' He said this to bring continuity with our last meeting. He then elaborated by saying, 'after leaving you, I decided to test all the three objectives of life. First I went into shares business to make quick money and use this money to enjoy life. But I was not really happy because this did not leave any time to reflect on more serious issues of life. Then I took the job of a manager in a private firm that gave me the opportunity to dominate people and get work extracted from them. Soon I got tired of this because this made me egoistic and vain. I found that I was hurting people more than helping them. It was then that I decided to join a religious organization to undergo the spiritual experience. This is how you see me in this attire and moving with religiously oriented people. I am now finding a peace of mind that I never had. It is leading me to an inner world that is probably as vast in mental domain as the outer world of sensuous experience but more rewarding. I feel I am becoming better as a human being with greater consciousness of my existence as a spiritual being and better appreciation of the mortal world of senses. But still I have to go along way in search of spiritual bliss that our scriptures talk of. It is giving me what I ventured to have and I believe now that truly it is a real purpose of life that saints and mystics have been telling us for centuries. There is a world of difference in the way a spiritually enlightened person sees the world and that an ordinary person of wealth or status thinks of. The material use of the world gives only temporary enjoyment and that too with associated problems of ego boost and unconcern towards others. To see every one in the same light has a charm of its own, that too without harming anyone. Spirituality does not change the person physically but gives a different direction to the way we see the objects in this world. It changes the way we look at people and interact with them. Humility, which is a characteristic of a spiritual person, is not a weakness but strength of character that disarms the most bullying type. You need to be brave enough to forgive others. This is my view after I have started the spiritual journey and traveled only the half way to the goal. I wish to go further and complete the journey.'

With this he stopped and went with fellow sadhus, leaving me to think whether the spiritual goal of enlightenment was the real objective of life. But I was happy that at least here was a man who decided to find the answer by his personal experience and did not leave it to others to decide for him.

THE ONE AND ONLY, SECOND TO NONE

In Vedantic parlance, the ultimate reality is abstract; the mere consciousness of being that is blissful. Whatever that entity is, it is the very substratum of existence. It is limitless in space and time, infinite and eternal, without any attributes of shape or size. This is how we visualize the reality in Nirakar form. But the same reality is seen with qualities in the Sakar form, qualities that we attribute to human like virtues, kind, loving, compassionate, helpful, creator, sustainer and destroyer, all powerful, all seeing, dispenser of justice and so on. Further we add that the same reality exists in both Nirakar and Sakar forms simultaneously. We further compound the picture by saying that it is the source of all things, the cause of creation and something that is beyond description. The reality is further stated to be the container of both the dual forms such as good and bad, light and heavy and so on.

In scriptures dealing with bhakti, we find thousand names of the same God Vishnu such as in Vishnusahastranam. These names are qualitative, in other words they qualify the God in terms of the qualities associated with Him. Similarly, qualitative descriptions are available for other forms of God. Even in Vedic descriptions, many qualitative descriptions appear for God. Swami Dayanand, in his book Satyarthprakash has given hundred names of God, which are qualitative in nature. In other religions too, we find many qualities assigned to God, such as all-merciful, all-powerful, invisible, loving, dispenser of justice etc. Is it our way of describing something that we do not understand fully or is it that an abstraction needs to be defined qualitatively to associate with? Whatever the reason, the multiquality God has come to stay in our vocabulary and firmly established as such in our memory.

If we take the scientific description of the reality, it is not difficult to accept an energy field that is present everywhere and takes on the material forms under specific conditions of energy concentration. Thus it becomes omnipresent and the cause of everything. The qualities associated are those of the form that it takes. As an energy field it is mathematically an abstraction. Its presence in infinite space-time continuum is a reality that exists. But the appreciation of this description needs specialized knowledge of higher mathematics. For ordinary persons, this knowledge is neither readily available nor understandable.

It is a fact that we tend to associate human like qualities to God, albeit at a much higher level, in order to make Him approachable and to be connected with our daily life. We want Him to be with us to sort out our problems, keep us on the right path and provide justice when we fail to get it through human resources. We need a supreme power to punish the guilty, and reward our good actions. We need a kind and compassionate touch of a supreme body that is Almighty. We need somebody to whom we can relate in our times of difficulty. It is a psychological need for reassurance. That is why somebody said that if there were no God, we would have to invent Him for our protection and praying to in times of difficulty. There is nothing wrong in this view if it helps people to be reassured. That is why, perhaps, an abstraction needs to be personalized for our own benefit.

THE SPIRITUAL DUTY

'When we come to this world we perform various duties that are obligatory in nature. We have duties towards our parents, towards spouse, and towards children that take away major part of our wakeful period of existence. There is however, one duty that we remain ignorant or unmindful of, that is towards us as human beings'

'What is that?'

'That is the spiritual duty towards our inner being. It is to find the true being of one's spiritual existence. It gives a higher direction to one's mind. It is the duty to have self-fulfillment. It is to free oneself from the binding forces of mundane existence. Fulfillment of this duty enlarges the consciousness and brightens the darkness of mind It is to experience the presence of God within, to establish a contact with God, to know one's powers hidden in the deep recesses of mind, to improve oneself at the subconscious level, and to develop wisdom that comes from the deeper self. It is not the wisdom that we associate with age but a wisdom that comes from inner enlightenment. It can come at any age but with required effort. It comes with meditation, carried out with patience and perseverance. It has a spiritual purpose in our life. This duty is the highest and all other duties are smaller in comparison. It is said that it is the prime duty and must be performed even at the cost of losing worldly happiness and sensuous enjoyment. The difficulty of doing this duty should not be a cause of neglecting it.'

'If it is so important, why is it that most people neglect it?'

'It is because either they are ignorant of it or are too scared to contemplate. We seem to have lost the art of contemplation in this modern age of fast life and stressful environment. We are so busy in mundane affairs that we hardly have any time to think of self-improvement in terms of inner wisdom, our obligation to society and enlightening our inner being. Man is eternally connected to God through the Holy Spirit. It is our duty to maintain this connection through enlarging our consciousness. Just as we feed the body with edible stuff, we need to feed our spirit the spiritual food of contemplation and meditation. The spiritual health of mind body complex is as important as the physical health of the body. Modern thinkers are now stressing this fact based on scientific results of experiments carried on brain functioning and the effect of mind on physical health. The isolation of mind and body is no longer valid in the studies on health care.'

'I do agree on the relevance of mind in the health care but we are talking of spirit that is different from mind.'

'Yes, you are right but mental health depends on the spiritual health. Unless our subconscious is clean, we shall continue to entertain evil thoughts that affect our mental health. Body, mind and spirit are intimately interconnected. We not only have to maintain physical body but also the mind and the spirit must be kept in good health. Neglecting one in comparison to the other is a bad policy. All the three are important to become a complete man.'

EVOLUTION AND SPIRITUALITY

Laws of morality and ethics arise from spiritual awareness. For example, seeing same God in every one is a spiritual experience. This gives a sense of equality, brotherhood, and concern for others because you find the same reality in all. Also, there is no sense in harming others when others are like you, harming them would be like harming yourself.

It is one's duty to learn the higher laws of existence through spiritual practice by expanding consciousness. The equality of all beings is seen in a higher plane of consciousness. Spirituality helps the evolution of society into a saner existence with concern for others as a basic principle of existence. Mere technological advancement is not enough to evolve. Making laws for peaceful coexistence and developing into a civilized society that cares for all is important too.

Improving personal and social conduct, a basic requirement for attaining spiritual experience, is important for creating a sense of social responsibility that is so necessary for civilized behavior. Spirituality is therefore directly linked to social evolution when it aims to improve the individual as an entity of collective behavior. Shedding greed and excessive acquisition is necessary for equitable distribution of resources. Spirituality has always emphasized the ill effects of greed and excessive acquisition as impediments for spiritual experience.

Spirituality is about individual discipline, freedom of self and universalism. It frees people of the fear of death. It expands the limit of consciousness to the very limit of the reality of existence. It concerns not only the outer world in ethics and morality but also the inner world of intuitive experience. It supports the evolution of complete man, in body, mind and spirit. It points the way to future maturing of human mind in sensuous and intuitive world.

The spiritual evolution of man lies in knowing what he is and why he is here. This spiritual awareness is vital to his evolution in consciousness as a human being. The solution to most problems in his life lies in answer to this. Generally these questions become more important in later life when a person takes stock of his life. It is never too late to delve in to this query and strive to find the answer.

The inner awakening is as important, or perhaps more, than the capacity to deal with the outer world. With inner strength of self-realization, one can deal with the problems of outer world in a much better way. Unless we learn to manage our thoughts, we cannot hope to find mental peace. Without this thought management our miseries in outer world are not going to fade away. We will remain engaged in trivialities and away from the truth of life. We blame others, our luck or even God because we do not know the true nature of our being. Without true knowledge of our self, we remain in the shadow of our ego and ignore the intuitive advice. Since the spiritual journey is long and arduous, it is important to know that even a few steps in this direction give their reward. Whatever is covered is not wasted. It helps to keep us on the path and brings its due reward as we march on.

LIFE OF HIGHER PURPOSE

Very few of us live with an aim of achieving something substantial either in material wealth or in spiritual advancement. Most of us live with daily routine of eating, sleeping and sensuous enjoyment as other animal species do. The wise of old have told us that mere survival is not the purpose of life. One has to have a higher purpose than mere survival.

To survive and be satisfied with the fulfillment of sensuous desires is stagnation. To have a higher purpose is being progressive. One of the higher purposes of life is the exploration of the inner being. This inner exploration leads to the reality of our existence, in fact of all creation. To merely exist or survive is hardly the correct use of human potential.

Professional or business success is important but it is not the primary aim of life. Spiritual attainment is necessary to rise above animalism. But out of 24 hours we are not even finding one hour for inner discovery. We are indeed misusing the time given to us for progress. Science has concentrated on investigations on matter, body and mind, but no effort is made to scrutinize the deeper levels of self, a study that is important for peace and harmony.

The justification for spiritual experience is the opening of divine possibilities that lie dormant in us. Personal happiness through temporary desire satisfaction in the material world is no substitute to the permanent bliss experienced through spiritual quest. The intuitive world is far more satisfying than the transitory sensuous experience.

Life without an ideal is without meaning. Without spiritual aspiration, the life is mechanical. The intellect may be needed for worldly affairs but it is the inner wisdom, or the intuitive thought, that brings spiritual success. To know that there are higher concepts and higher values in life that need to be acquired, gives hope to those who have missed peace and tranquility in their life in the pursuit of material success.

There are some who consider the higher concepts and higher values of life as the preoccupation of the neurotics, not knowing themselves that these constitute the very foundation of life. The higher purpose of raising consciousness towards supreme power is a step towards divinity, a realization of the unity with God.

It is wrong to say that realization of self is a selfish act. The self-realization works for the betterment of those who come in contact with the enlightened one. It is also wrong to dismiss mysticism as an escape from worldly problems. It seeks and realizes the inner reality. For that very purpose, it is worth pursuing even if the person ignores the material world. Frauds and cheats sometimes indulge in mysticism to their selfish ends, but that is no reason to denounce it as a purpose in life. In purity it is hard work involving study and meditation; with high degree of honesty, kindness, love and concern for others. This changes our view of life and makes a connection with the inner reality.

LIVING FOR PROGRESS AND PROSPERITY

'Is it justified to say that we come to this earth to generate wealth, create a family and do our duties to them and vanish like other animals? Is this the ideal we live for and die?'

'For most people this is what that makes them live This way they continue the species and that is what nature wants them to do. Principles, values and knowledge and skill are the work of man too that civilizes the man and puts additional stress on living generation. If you want more, you are probably living in imaginative world where extrasensory activities and miracles are expected of you.'

'You probably did not get my point. Is there no higher purpose to life than mere procreation and sensuous enjoyment? I would have expected you to mention at least that in spite of the best efforts of man, he has not been able to banish suffering from this world. Alleviation of misery and suffering would at least be a desired objective for some inspired persons.'

'In my view that is already taken care of by the generation of wealth through hard work and advancement of technology.'

'If that were so, there would be no suffering in rich and advanced countries which have evolved a system of economic management whereby every body is able to provide for himself enough resources for a good physical life. I thought there was more to life than simply commerce and economics. I thought happiness is a product of both body and mind and mere physicality alone cannot account for mental peace and spiritual desires.'

'You are not justified to ignore or downgrade the importance of prosperity in human happiness. You have to live in poverty to know this truth.'

'I know prosperity is important to meet physical demands, but it is not the sole criterion for mental peace. I would expect you to appreciate that hard work and ceaseless activity for wealth generation are not conducive to growth of peace and tranquility in growing societies. A continuously busy and agitated mind does not provide peace, howsoever intelligent the person may be. Mental peace requires a serene atmosphere, a still mind and a desire free temperament. You cannot buy peace with wealth and prosperity. At best you can be free of the worries connected with your mundane desires, but peace of mind results from a shift in attitude. Spiritual outlook is imperative for permanent peace in mind. So long as fulfillment of desires is the objective of life, mental peace will always be elusive.'

'It is all very well to sermonize on the spiritual aspects but the practicality of life is different. Poverty is the biggest factor in agitating the mind. And poverty cannot be removed without hard work for wealth generation. An empty stomach cannot think of spiritual practices. Such luxuries as adoption and practice of higher aims of life are possible only in a wealthy society. The growth of art and advancement of science are possible in stable and richer nations that allow sustained efforts by the well to do.'

'While there is some truth in what you say, it is not entirely correct to say that spirituality as a higher aim cannot prosper in poverty. The life of great saints is a testimony to the fact that most saints were without material wealth and even if given the choice of riches they spurned the offer and opted to remain without wealth and comfort that we crave. They were people with dedication to their cause of uplifting others to the level of their consciousness. They lived by their aim of spreading awareness of spiritual reality and wanted every one to experience the inner light. It is their example that lights our path to divinity. They experimented and found the inner truth and spread their message of higher purpose.'

'I do concede that spiritual experience has its own merits but every one cannot follow their example of piety, simplicity and pecuniary sacrifice. It takes some courage of conviction to follow in their footsteps. One has to change one's concept of enjoyment, if one wants to adopt their kind of life. The saints and mystics are made of a different stuff. They live in intuitive world and most of them severe their worldly connections. Their preaching also exhorts others to detach from the material world and connect with the intuitive reality. Let us face it, the modern world runs on money. That is why you find so many religious teachers arrange paid courses in spirituality. The old ideas about spiritual life must take into consideration the changed environment and should modify spiritual teaching that is relevant to the business like living of today. In this fast paced consumerist society, high ideals must compromise with practicality of comfortable living. By all means have a lofty aim but be practical to know the limitations imposed by market oriented life.'

'You are almost conceding my point that a high aim is important to seek satisfaction in life. Wealth, though important, is not the source of happiness.

Fulfillment of higher aim is order of magnitude more satisfying than routine wealth generation, and enjoyment of senses thereof. Philosophers, saints and mystics have realized this fact in their life and have preached any number of times. Let us reflect on that and decide. Life is precious and it cannot be squandered away on trivial activities that are of no consequence in shaping the future.'

ONE AND MANY

God is one but sages know Him by different names
God is one but religions and gods are many
God is one but people worship Him in many ways
God is one but scriptures are many
God is one but paths to Him are many

God is without attributes, but people know Him by qualities assigned
The Spirit is nondual, but people know It through manifold manifestations
The ultimate Reality and the spirit in man are no different, but seen differently by people
My God and yours are no different, but religions make it so
The paths of all places of worship meet at the door of God
God listens to the faintest murmur of prayer if it comes from pure heart

REMINISCENCES

THE QUEST

His close friends and parents called him Vicky because his full name was too long. He was by no means extraordinary by any standard of judgment. He was an introvert from childhood; he never mixed with strangers even when there was an occasion to do so. This made him rather aloof in a crowd. His family background was partly responsible for this oddity; he had lost his father when he was hardly four. He saw the world as if he was watching a fair all by himself and had no resources to take part in any game. He had learnt to ignore others, and suppress his desires, from an early age, but his keen sense of observation enabled him to accumulate worldly knowledge that he hardly used. He was a loner and he preferred to remain so.

For his timidity and humility, his friends tried to patronize him. He was however, sharp in his studies. His intellect and hard work carried him comfortably through the school till he faced the competition in professional studies where the cream of the country vied for a seat. Then he knew how varied the world was. It became clear to him that in this world, no one could claim the extraordinary status without extraordinary talents and hard work. He then knew that he was among the equals and many times even felt inferior to some of his colleagues. In school he went through the pangs of growing out of adolescence and became aware of his adult hood in the college. However, he kept his cool and did not share his thoughts with any one. His introvert nature helped him to keep his thoughts to himself. He did not share his problems with anyone either. Though he came from an ordinary middle class family, a teacher's son, his pride kept him away from looking like a deprived person. He liked to dress well with whatever he had. Though he did not have an athletic body, he played cricket with enthusiastic vigor and interest. The occasional success in the game satisfied his ego, which he enjoyed thoroughly.

He was a vegetarian and a teetotaler. In parties he was a nonentity. He rarely liked to introduce himself. He talked when talked to. But when he came onto the subject of his likeness, he was difficult to stop. He did not realize that in parties people exchange pleasantries as a formality and it is indecent to remain silent when others are chattering about non-issues. He was, in that context, a simpleton, but a person with good heart and kind nature. He did not bear ill will to anyone. Even in competition, he did not mind being outwitted by his less talented colleagues who knew the ways of the world. In a sense this made him a misfit in the company of cheats and cunning ones. His confidence in his inherent ability however, kept him alive and successful in his academic life. His interest in learning enabled him to collect quite a few degrees. Though he lacked financial resources, his hard work and government scholarships carried him through to earn a professional degree and become a successful engineer. But in tune with his temperament, he liked to do research work more than the practical applications.

I have always felt that success brings enemies. Vicky had his share of setbacks and jolts in his professional life. His friends always thought that his success was unjustified. Though this attitude of some of his friends angered him occasionally, he soon learnt to recover from this depressing thought and carried on with his usual pace of work. He did this with the sense of detachment worthy of a philosopher.

One day, a friend of his, was very angry on some trivial point. Vicky told him, 'why are you so angry at life? The life is to enjoy and learn the lessons. In fact, the whole purpose of coming to life is to learn the lessons of life through interactions with other living beings; shedding the negative emotions and become a positive person.' This remark however was not appreciated by his friend because he thought how could a nonentity like Vicky could advise him when he enjoyed a greater status and presumably more intelligence than Vicky. All that Vicky could say in defense was that it is always better to lower one's pride if you want to be happy.

In the middle years of his life span, the loss of some close relatives saddened him and he turned more inward looking. He tried to find the reasons and rationale of pain that strikes like a bolt to even the righteous. This at times, propelled him to atheism as a sign of anger towards God. But eventually he turned to religion because his earlier training at home had told him to believe in God that promises everlasting joy and happiness. It was as if faith provided escape from fate. Out of sheer desperation he turned to scriptures for finding the answers to 'why the pious and righteous suffer when the crooked and cunning prosper?'

In psychiatric parlance, the highly introverted persons are odd balls in a heap of normal ones. Those who reject society are either having a complex or lack the ability to adjust with the normal ones. In that respect they lie almost at the fringe of lunacy. They need therefore, in their opinion, the medical care and advice. I am not competent to comment on that since I am not a specialist in mental disorders. But I do believe that it is the odd balls who are creative and path breakers that have carried forward the legacy of science, philosophy and religion. The introverted persons are inclined to develop a reading habit because they find books as their best friends. The books provide them the company they need for relaxation and advice.

Coming back to the life of Vicky, whenever something unpleasant happens in our life we start blaming God or fate, as if our own actions have nothing to do with it. This tendency comes from not knowing the true identity of God. This happened with Vicky when within a short span he lost two dear and loveable persons and had a tiff with his boss. In our growing environment, we are taught that God controls every event in our life. Therefore whatever happens we assign the responsibility of that to God. We forget that chance events, accidents and unexpected events do happen in every one's life. God is not supervising our life. It is our own accumulated actions and our free will that control the happenings in our life. But this understanding is forgotten in moments of extreme sadness and bereavements. A lack of true knowledge about God is also responsible for such a state. Vicky felt the pressure of events and lost his cool.

One day he asked a friend, 'why is this happening to me when I have, to the best of my knowledge, not harmed any one'. He took God to be some kind of superintendent that disbursed awards and punishment to his juniors and liable to be partial in his dealings. It was a strange attitude for a person of his temperament and learning. This is where a clash between emotions and intellect occurs and a person untrained in spirituality goes haywire. His friend however, consoled him by saying that he was not the only person in this world to face such a situation and many like him have gone through the same situation because there are some things for which there are no clear-cut answers and there is no option but to bear it with courage and move forward. But Vicky kept in his mind the shock and decided to find the answer at a later date.

As we know time heals but slowly. The shock of losing someone dear and close is an impulse of negative energy that dissipates over a time till you regain your composure and start living afresh. The same happened to Vicky. He started taking interest in his professional duties and remaining family. Slowly he regained the confidence and thought of improving his personal life to a level where comfort and joy replaced agony and helplessness. He improved his living environment with a new house and absorbed himself in gardening. He developed faith in life and God afresh. He started believing in the cyclic way of joy and sorrow, a peak of happiness followed by a dip of unhappiness, a sort of sine curve, with a frequency varying with the individual concerned.

Time passes swiftly in comfort but drags on in difficulty. The undulations in the circumstances keep a person engaged and he forgets the purpose of life till again a jolt comes to remind him that life has a purpose. Two more jolts and he was back to thinking about the drama of life in which he was caught as an unwilling player. This time he took the religion seriously and started reading with a mission to find answers to the questions that bothered him from time to time. He wanted to know what sages wrote about life, God and the spiritual way of life that promised eternal bliss.

He did not know at that time that generally we make a mistake of taking the scriptures literally because our level of consciousness is different from that of sages when they expressed their spiritual experiences. They were seeing life in a different perspective than what we do in this time. They lived in the jungles of wood while we live in the jungles of concrete. They had plenty of time for introspection and meditation while we seldom think of other than our routine life of money, prestige and safety. The differential in time as well as the difference in consciousness is significant. But one thing is common. It is that of concern with happiness and sorrow. When Vicky read them, he went into a different world. He was amazed to see their search for truth that put them face to face with the ultimate reality. He realized that a different world existed beyond the one in which most mortals lived and suffered. That world was the inner world as against the outer world of sense objects. The inner world was calm and free while the sense world was full of fear, worries and bonded attachment.

He also studied the religious philosophers to know whether their wisdom was right in the present context. Were the sages talking of timeless wisdom? Were they right in saying that our senses could not see the reality of existence? Were they right in claiming that what we see with our eyes is not the whole truth? Was the truth different from what we believed in? He tried to relate the sage's conclusion with the modern truth shown by science. It was a painful exercise since the truth of science did not agree with religious truth all the way, though at one point they agreed. We in material form differed from our reality in spiritual sense. At the level of ultimate reality, all existence was one and all humans were part of that oneness.

To understand the scriptures correctly, he thought it necessary to raise his level of consciousness as is prescribed in the various techniques and procedures associated with rise of spirituality. He had not only to focus his thoughts on the revelations about reality in scriptures but also go through practices of meditation on that reality. Slowly, the meaning of what he read became clear. As he read more and more, along with the practice of meditation, the scriptures became clearer and he could develop his interest more. It is a common feeling that more you become adept the more you become interested in the subject. He not only read the words but also deliberated on them to make out the sense and context in which the words were written. He read the commentaries on the original texts by the celebrated authors and tried to link one text with the other to make the point clear. All this reading was assimilated with the history of the period in which the texts were written so as to correlate the social context of the times in which the revelations were made. As Vicky told me, it was a great experience that left a deep impression on his psyche. At times he felt spellbound by the revelations of the great masters of spiritual experience. For days he deliberated on them and compared his spiritual findings with his background of science to see what was the truth. Slowly he could find some correlation up to a point. But a great gulf still remained to be bridged.

This exercise of finding commonality between science and spirituality continued for over a decade till he found the essential difference between the two streams. He found that religion started where science ended. Spirituality had nothing to do with materialism, which was the foundation of enquiry in science. Further, he found that intellect had a role up to a point and no further in stepping the ladders of spirituality. The direct route to spiritual experience lay in the feeling of love for God and His creation. It was not possible to experience God with intellect, though you could know the identity of God through that. But experience and knowing are two different things. Science may tell you the ultimate reality but it cannot make you experience it. Knowing through a book is different from conducting an experiment. Similarly, the experience is different from mere knowledge. Spirituality is about experiencing the reality of existence. He found that creative energy was present universally but experiencing that energy, as a potent force, was possible only through the spiritual route.

As a result of his struggle with his enquiring mind, he came to certain conclusions about life and how to live life without getting unnecessarily bogged down with unanswerable questions. A calm descended on him when he realized that certain things are beyond space and time and it is only through faith that you can approach them. It was a turning point in his life. He felt relieved mentally and changed his attitude towards his life and towards others. He saw God present in all living beings as much as in him. The reality was a form of conscious energy and that existed in all beings. What differed were the consequences of our actions from one person to another. And that made all the difference that confuses us all. God had nothing to do with our fortune or our misery. It was totally unjust to blame God for our failings. Every one could rise to the highest levels of spiritual existence that we named as God. Actions follow the law of reaction and hence the unexpected events in our life. Whatever happens in our life is of our own making; if not in this life it could be an accumulated storehouse of reactions that need to express sometime without our knowledge. We make our destiny and blame God for it.

Every moment in our life we learn through interaction with the outside world. But the purpose of life is to learn spiritual lessons in life that is given to us by nature. Religious philosophers have told us that life is a mechanism to learn lessons that enable us to rise in consciousness.

Caught between science and religion, because of his background of science and tilt towards religion, Vicky found that his attitude to life had changed; he had become more tolerant to disagreement, and his emotional life leaned towards love for all and hatred for none; though off and on he succumbed to these negative emotions, but overall he felt that he had improved himself for the better. He had learnt never to fail in returning a favor and to never feel proud before his relatives and elder ones. He was eager to develop the traits like love, compassion, charity, faith, and forgiveness and not to resort to any kind of violence.

His studies in spirituality taught him to unlearn fear, hatred, anger, violence, greed, pride, lust, selfishness and prejudices. The list of negative emotions also included guilt, shame, sadness, anxiety, worry, and envy that clouded his blissful soul. Loving relationships were the most effective tools for learning the positives and unlearning the negative ones. In this connection one could recall the learning of a child from his/her mother. Further, he noted that learning and unlearning was best done through experience rather than mere reading of books or scriptures. The emotional experience and intellect do not mix. While intellect helps to interact with the outside world for the growth of body and mind, it is love that takes one to spiritual experience. He also learnt that it is more important to learn how to treat a person than gaining or losing from that person. It became apparent to him that when you find the same God residing in all human hearts, you reach a higher level of consciousness. Spirit is free while sense objects are binding. To be free from the bondage of worldly temptations, the most important factor is the freedom from fear of death. This fear is the root cause of worry and anxiety in relationships and worldly interactions. Further, the label of religion is not important; what really matters is the personal experience of spiritual uplift and raising the level of consciousness rather than getting bogged down in the web of rituals and external aspects of labeled religions. Vicky found that the most important aspect of every religion was to see God in every object of creation and feel a sense of equality with all humanity. He realized that to be spiritual, it is not necessary to be a great man of position and wealth, but it is to be a good man, even though ignored by the elite of society.

From his personal experience of life, when he suffered at the hands of others, he learnt that the negative feelings of anger, hatred and revenge affect the body and mind more to the aggrieved than the cause of it. It is now established as a scientific fact that stress of any kind is injurious to human body and causes many ailments through various secretions in the body. Anger therefore hurts the angry more than the one who causes it. Anger arises from failure in expectations and fear of failure and loss of esteem. A little wisdom and love for others can generate the understanding and avoid the bad effects. To rise in spirituality, the negative emotions serve as the roadblocks, which have to be overcome with patience and understanding.

What is the objective behind this process of learning? Vicky learnt from his religious friends that the object of life was to attain a higher level of consciousness and climb the ladder of intuitive awareness, a process that goes on even after physical death. But being a person pf inquisitive mind, he was not much convinced. The materialists told him that there was no such thing as life after death. Being caught between these two extremes, he was not sure what was the objective of life. However, he was convinced that learning experiential lessons was good for self as well as for the society. It brought peace of mind to the individual and stability to the society. He was convinced that an unbridled mind was like the untrained horse that could run wild.

His introspection and analysis of the experiences made him a person of understanding. He could now face difficulties with fortitude and hindsight. A dawn of wisdom was appearing in his life that he considered as a gift of God for all the vicissitudes he faced in life. He was now coming to the conclusion that life is meant to live and learn so that we rise in our consciousness. It was necessary to appreciate the purpose of nature and become a partner in its intelligence to divinize the whole existence. It did not matter if we were the fist to learn or the last to do so. What mattered was the elevation in mental evolution. As Aurobindo pointed out, the whole purpose of nature is to rise in consciousness to the level of divinity. It does not matter at what time scale it happens. The achieving of objective is all that matters. The humanity plays an important role in this venture because it is the most evolved species. It is incumbent on us to take the whole humanity to the heights of universal existence both in mind and body. The alternative is too dangerous for its existence. If we do not utilize our brain, the highest object of evolution, properly, the alternative is degradation and extinction. The brain's capacity, along with principles of spirituality, can lift us to unimaginable heights, which at present we ascribe only to divine existence.

A DUTIFUL MOTHER

Mothers are known for the love for their children, the difficulties they face for the sake of comfort and well being of their loved ones and the concern they show for their growth. But I am not talking now of this aspect, which is well known to all. I wish to tell another quality that I found in a mother that is not so common, in fact rarely found. This is about the love of a mother where she not only loved and cared for her own children but also those of other mothers, the common factor being the father.

She was woman of regal appearance, calm and composed, radiating a look of compassion and understanding. No body could feel angry before her. She was religious in the conventional sense of the term, though she came from a background where idol worship was discouraged. She was pious and loving to all those who looked up to her for help. Even though she became a widow at the young age of thirty-five, she never wavered in her piety and righteous living. When her husband died, she was left with six children to support and look after with the meager salary of a primary school teacher. The eldest was yet to pass his high school exam. After a year though, he joined her in taking the responsibility for the upbringing of the younger ones. She was indeed both a father and mother to all the children who were her responsibility. The children adored her and looked to her for every thing.

There is a theory, though not proved, that sufferance comes to good persons as divine intervention to wash off their Karma. Whatever be the reason, she was certainly the victim of this strange belief. She had barely settled in her job when a family problem descended on her. It tested her courage and patience but she came out successfully out of it. We know that problems multiply with each addition to the family. And she had six of them to care for. With her meager resources and no relative to support, it was a life full of strife and concern. All the six had to be educated so that they could stand on their own. She was a firm believer in the gender equality. She worked hard to provide equal opportunity in education to her daughters as well as the sons.

Time passed but slowly in difficult circumstances. Many times she felt lonely in this fight against poverty and needs. But her own *samskaras* were good and she gave good *samskaras* to her children. The net effect was that there was full cohesion in the family and a determination to fight the scarcity and deprivation. God in turn helped by providing intelligence to the children who in turn earned scholarships for study ahead. It was a family lacking in resources but abundant happiness through love and understanding.

Ultimately a time came when her children completed education and got into jobs. But destiny follows surreptitiously. Soon the daughter in law problem set in. Being a lady of good nature, she could not read the world correctly. She was literally conned into relationships she never deserved. The sons being powerless before their wives, she was cornered into a situation where she had no choice but to isolate herself from those on whom she had showered everything that she had. It was indeed sad to see her feeling so lonely, at times one lost faith in humanity.

She was so used to setbacks that she accepted this last one bravely and with fortitude. She was rather philosophical in her last days. She asked me once where does a person go after death. I had no answer then. But now I feel if ever there is a heaven, it must be for persons like her, who so selflessly devote their best years in their life to the service of those who deny any reward whatsoever in return. If at all there is a God, He cannot be so unjust as to deny a place of honor for such persons.

What tribute can one give to such a lady, except that you stand in silence and respect her selfless work and admire her patience and understanding? For those who believe in the benevolence of God, it is nothing short of the work of God's messenger to help the needy. It is not justified to think that the messengers of God come with wings to help the weak and the helpless. If and when they come, they come in human form as ordinary persons with whom we can relate to. They love us and solve our problems of daily life and guide us to a bright future. They need no reward and no recognition. Such persons are described as true karamyogis in the spiritual parlance.

Millions come and millions go
Rarely ever the world remembers them
It is only a few who leave an imprint
On the minds of those left behind

Should we call them angels or guides?
Should we pay obeisance to them?
Or should we simply remember them
As the benefactor of needy souls

They are the gift of God
To those that are born with destiny not too good
They come to make others' life worthwhile
That otherwise would have been wasted out

We call them stars that shine above the earth
We stare at stars that shine in films and sports
We are in awe of those who are wealthy and wise
But we never respect those that suffer in silence for us

We are an ungrateful lot

For we live for ourselves
And remember not those
That gave us all

THE RENUNCIANT

She was a model of selfless work that we find only mentioned in scriptural literature. She was at heart as soft and pure as the fresh white snow. She was a bubbly girl in the child hood. In a big family she did not get the attention that was due to her. But she had dreams as vibrant as any girl of her age would have. She loved every one in the family, her mother, her brothers and sisters, both elder and younger to her. You would wonder why I did not mention the father. It is because she lost her father in young age when she was under ten years. At that time she did not realize the importance of losing her father. But at a later stage she missed him very much because she knew from her childhood memories that he loved her very much. When she wanted his love and affection in her life it was just not available to her. This made her sad and introverted. But she was a brave girl.

Adolescence is a period of dreams and difficulty in growth. It is a period of dreams about the future, dreams about romance, a successful life and a pleasant family life. But at the same time, it is a period of hard work to achieve one's aims and fulfillment of dreams. The person lives in a world that is more imaginative than real. There is pressure of studies, combined with a desire to fly and experience the world. But how many can fulfill their dreams in later life. It is not entirely a question of self-effort. The circumstances of family, the individual's capacity to cope up with stresses of society, the environment of bringing up all add up to present conditions that may or may not be conducive to achieve the aims. But it is a period of change, both physically and mentally.

She also faced the difficult adolescence and looked chirpy and vibrant. But her fate had a different agenda. Her destiny had to teach her a lesson that she would live forever in the rest of her life. Her dreams of romance nose-dived when she found that the person she loved had taken fancy for another. This broke her heart and she cursed her luck. She decided not to marry again, a decision she stuck to with calm determination and firm resolve. Every one knows from personal experience that it is a very difficult thing to suppress emotions of love in youth. But she steadfastly stood her ground with piety and grim resolve. For most people in this situation this becomes a burden; but she turned this setback to her strength. It later became her strength of character by changing her priorities in life.

She decided to work for others and help even those who caused her hurt. She decided to spend her income from salary and savings on her relatives, acquaintances and even those she knew who were out to exploit her charitable disposition. She lived the life of simplicity, honesty and devotion, rarely going for her own happiness and pleasure. Even if she purchased an item that she liked, she soon donated to those who expressed the need of that. She always put others comfort above her own. She could not see any body suffering, even if the suffering was of that person's own doing.

The world however, rarely understands such persons. They have no sympathy with the plight of such tender hearts and unashamedly tend to exploit them for their own ends. When she fell ill, no one came to her help. She suffered in silence. Many of those who benefited from her paid only lip sympathy.

There is one thing about religion that interests me and touches me to the core. When a virtuous and kind person finds that his/her near and dear ones have lost interest in him/her because the person has nothing more to benefit them, it is God that becomes an anchor to that person. He or she finds solace in religion, shares his/her feelings with God and starts devoting more and more time to thoughts concerning the Divine. Some may say it is an escapist attitude, but to the person it is the only platform that provides a feeling of love and concern to the individual. The same happened to the girl that I am writing about. Slowly, when she found that her capacity to help had grown weak because of her own circumstances, her relations and her close friends turned their faces away, leaving her with a loneliness she found quite disturbing and at times unbearable. She then turned to God, not knowing exactly what God meant. To her it was only a faith in the personal God that kept her alive and sane. She had no house to stay, no one to call as her own, no one who could provide shelter and protection in her times of difficulty and illness. Her inner strength and her salary kept her going with greater and greater leanings towards God. She spent her free time in temples and discourses and even serving in holy places to get personal satisfaction out of this worldly life. I think even an atheist would not object to this anchoring role of God. I am saying this because I have seen this happen.

It is an irony of some sort that even in the name of God, we do things that God would not approve of. She was indeed duped by a well-known institution doing charitable work She deposited a major part of her earnings in that institution with the hope that they would provide her the shelter and protection in her later years when she will not have the strength to cope up with this world. But to her surprise, when the time came, she was denied the facility on the premise that her money was only a donation and not for the purpose, which she had supposed. But her good nature ignored this shock and went on working to save again for the rainy day.

With all the surprises that this world bestowed on her, her belief in the religious piety and good intentions never wavered. She remained a staunch believer in the goodness of human beings. She believed all friends and foes and gave her all whenever any one demanded a favor or some help to accomplish their task. She was a living example of saintly attitude towards others. She answered a rebuke with a smile. Even if she knew that somebody was deceiving her, she ignored the hurt and helped the person thinking that the person needed help. What hurt me was that the world never returned her favors and continued to fleece her taking the advantage of her simple and frank disposition that never differentiated between the good and the bad. This trait is rarely seen these days of selfish dealings and greedy acquisitions.

Why am I telling all this? It is because persons like her are being tainted as foolish and naive in the present environment of stealing, snatching and self-aggrandizement. We are putting such people at a disadvantage in society and thereby dissuading others to follow such behavior. Our heroes are villainous in character because we think cheating is an art. We hail those who have risen in life through maneuverings and influence. A simple, honest and straightforward life is seen as a loser's life. We want to grow tall by suppressing the shoulders of others. Success has become synonymous with cunning, dishonesty and deception.

A LIFE GONE WRONG

In countries, on the path of liberalism on the lines of western culture, particularly in the west and east of Asia, conservatism coexists with neo liberalism. You find love marriages happening as frequently as the arranged marriages. A debate rages between the two schools of thought as to what is better in the long run. The pro love marriage argument stresses the independence of the two minds exercising their rights to choose since they have to live together. Those against love marriages argue that parents out of love for their children like to use their worldly wisdom to choose the right partner for their child.. As to the divorce between the estranged couples, there is nothing much to choose between the two methods of finding the spouse. However, in love marriages the partners know each other before they plunge into the bond. In the arranged case, the love blossoms, albeit slowly, but lingers on for a longer time. In many cases though, the love factor matures to tolerance and acceptance of each other and life moves like a car traveling on a rough road. Some of these unfortunate ones resign to fate, while others decide to end the association for better companions.

I know two cases where the journey proved not a pleasure but a tough one to carry on.

The first one concerns a darling little boy who was handsome and good looking and smart enough to play pranks on other family members. He was intensely liked by his mother who dotted on him. He was good in his studies and showed promise for becoming the star of the family. The family being short of finances, all looked up to him to become the pillar of support in times to come. He was loving and obedient. He was a good swimmer, and indulged in hobbies of doing experiments in electronic gadgetry, even when in school. His desire was to become an electronics engineer, but as luck would have it, this opportunity was denied to him. He had scored very high in main subjects but due to carelessness; his marks in subsidiary subjects were low, resulting in the total going below requirement for admission to the engineering courses. This put him off for some time but then he regained his confidence and did his master's in pure science with flying colors.

To make a career, one needs, not only a good ranking in exams but also good advice too. There was no body in the family to advise him properly. The result was that he landed in a job where promotions were far and few and the work involved not much intellectual input but only a physical effort. This disappointed him immensely, for his ambition to contribute to professional success did not materialize to the extent he wanted. Soon, he developed an attitude of complacency towards life and became quietly tolerant.

His marriage was another disaster waiting to happen. His job required him to go on long trips to wild areas, which meant long periods of separation from his wife. This took a toll on his married life and a sense of bitterness evolved in marital relationship. To add to his woes, the couple remained childless that generated further bitterness in life. He felt as if God cheated him, and his faith in Him waned. Though he belonged to a staunchly religious family, his belief system got a jolt due to his personal problems. Due to constant worries of personal and professional nature, he developed psychosomatic disease, which multiplied his worries. He became concerned with his future and became dejected.

Strange are the ways a life moves on. In fact every person's life can make a good novel if written in a literary style. The same happened to his life when after a long spell of dissatisfaction in profession; he landed in a good teaching job in a prestigious institution. The life moved smoothly, though the absence of a child remained a sore point of dissatisfaction. He even improved academically by writing books and obtaining higher qualification. His family was happy because he was settled at one place, and did not have to move every now and then to long trips to wild and isolated places. He went abroad on teaching assignments, which brought him honor and respect.

After a while, he felt his health was showing signs of deterioration. But he took it in his stride and went on living cheerfully. He went on holidays abroad to enjoy since he had suffered enough in the past. His wife supported him to cope with his life of bad health, but with advancing years he felt lonely inside. He was fond of reading and music, but now he felt he could no longer enjoy these diversions because his illness came in between his happiness and illness. He felt that all these times, due to his own problems, he had neglected his mother who doted on him. He felt quite helpless and knew that he was not repaying his mother's love to her. This is a situation that can only be felt and not expressed..

I met him from time to time to know how he was progressing in life. Many times I felt sorry for him because I felt the destiny had deprived him the happiness and joy that he had a claim to, because of his intelligence and hard work that he had put in. But destiny had its own role to play. Though we say that a person makes his/her own destiny, we tend to neglect the fact that there are times when even with good intentions, our actions go wrong. His religion told him that it was the accumulated actions of past life that formed the destiny. But the bitterness he faced in life made him angry with God. In one of my meetings with him he categorically stated that there was no soul and no God. Perhaps he formed this view because of his experience in the west where a different philosophy ruled. Looking at his life, I wondered many times as to what was the truth. Was life purely an accident by which we came to have material bodies with a beating heart and thinking brain? Or was there more to it? Now of course I hold a different view after having read somewhat more on the religious and scientific views on life. In a way it is good that we do not know our past and future. If we did know, the life would become unbearable with anxiety and expectations.

The last time I saw him, he was very dejected because his illness had aggravated and he could not indulge in his favorite time pass of reading and writing. He was writing his last book when his eyes failed him. He needed help badly but having no one to come forward, it was a torture to live, just sitting without any action, neither thinking nor doing anything physical. His wife gave him company by sitting beside him. It was becoming pitiable just watching him deteriorate.

One day a call came to me that he needed help. I went and found him sinking. He was moved to a nearby hospital where he continued to sink. Within twenty-four hours the doctors gave up hope and he departed on a long journey in spirit form. I felt within myself a deep sense of anguish since I kept wondering why a promising life ended the way it did. But I found no answer except that it is the way of life. The promises and the actual happenings never come together, except when the divine desires so. Call it fate or divine will, but this is the reality we all have to face.

The other case is of a 'she'. It is similar to the first in the sense that it too reflects the interference of fate in the promising hope of a good life. But here too the childhood hopes were belied and a tragic end ensued. She was born under happy circumstances and the fortunetellers had predicted that she would live like a queen. But astrology, like the other science of forecasting, is like weather forecasting without any scientific tools. The prediction, wherever it comes true, is purely accidental. Normally, the prediction is at best intuitive. She spent her childhood in happy circumstances but by the time she entered adolescence, the family fortunes had declined. The situation became so bad that it came down to a hand to mouth living. Her father made a fatal mistake of resigning the government job and entering into business for which he had neither the experience nor the aptitude. He was an emotional person, prone to believe his subordinate for which he paid a heavy price. The business was doomed to failure before it even took off. The result was a heavy loss and consequent problems for the family.

The shock of the financial decline, multiplied with family problems, took toll on his health and he departed from this world in middle age. Luckily, her mother, who was a lady of great courage and character, took up the challenge and raised the family with determination and hard work. She took up the job of a schoolteacher, and supported by the elder son, managed to keep the family and financial needs growing. This enabled the younger ones to get their food and education and grow into healthy citizens in body and mind.

However, children have their own dreams. They want to enjoy life and have hopes of growing into power and wealth. But when the reality of life bites, their dreams are shattered. They come to know then that there are forces at work, which come in the way of their fulfilling the dreams. This is the first sign of learning and becoming wise about the world. One can put in hard work but one cannot override circumstances beyond one's control. With all her intelligence, and the zeal for achievement of her goal, she found herself helpless before the prevailing lack of financial resources. Therefore she had to compromise on her aims of college education and a good job. All that she could manage was a diploma and a teaching assignment that could carry her through in later life.

Though she married in love and hoped to live a happy life, her husband's vocation again forced her to compromise on her financial demands. Though she expected from life a royal living, all she got was a life of lower middle class that hardly satisfied her. But her intelligence and common sense made her realize her situation and she made peace with what she had. Humans have a great sense of adaptability, and sooner or later every one comes to the level of existence where survival instinct forces one to adjust. This is why, not only she but her children too, had to adjust to the available resources and accept the pecuniary reality with controlled desires. Whenever I met them, I felt sorry for the kids but could hardly alter the situation.

It is an old saying that adversity brings out the best in a person. The same happened to her. She collected all her courage and stood to face the problems with worldly wisdom and determination. Slowly things started moving and her daughters also started helping her. However, she had the misfortune of her only son remaining a liability for he neither showed any interest in studies nor helped her otherwise. To add to her misfortune, he married against her will and separated from the family.

To compound the problem, her married daughter, who was a great help to her emotionally in all her difficulties, passed away, leaving the two children to her care. The son in law married again. Her grit and faith in herself kept her going and she managed to run the family smoothly. But her misfortune still did not leave her. Her husband passed away leaving her shattered for she loved him intensely. One or two family members came to her help, but it was only for a short time. She was reduced to a mechanical life and her routine worked like a machine. She lost all faith in divine and lived only to bring up her grand sons. She often wondered why God is so severe with people who want to live a simple life without troubling others. But such questions have no answers. For a person immersed in deep waters, there is no rescue but to try to come up only to breathe. For them death is a great relief.

After a struggle to exist for over half a century, the promising child became a living corpse. Lying in a hospital for nearly two long years, she expired. The two grandsons were reduced to the status of orphans in order to keep the struggle going. I was witness to her last rites, full of grief and sorrow, and wondered if this was the life God meant us to live. People say that life is full of ups and downs. But for many it means only ups while for others it means only downs. One thing that stood up in her life was her independence of thought and action and facing the problems single-handedly without asking any kind of assistance. She was a brave lady in that sense. She did not even want any help from God for she had full confidence in her capacity to face the downs of life. I could only salute her courage of conviction and strength of character in living a life that most people will dread to face. May God rest her soul in peace for she had enough of action in her life in this world.

The unevenness of pain and pleasure among people of same background is very difficult to explain except on the Karma theory. Though it looks logical, yet one does not know for what actions of previous life the person is being punished. This generates a sense of bitterness that makes one lose faith in God and divine dispensation. Even the theory of chance and probability would not venture to prove the facts of one's life. Why would the probability of sufferance be more in one case and not the other? Why only some persons are picked up for sufferance. May be, I am getting extra sensitive to her case but these incidents make one wonder. In the absence of any rational explanation, people turn to speculative answers and become superstitious. They resort to all sorts of unrational activities to avoid unpleasantness in life.

This case is not unique but only a typical example of all those sufferers who hardly see the fun in life. There are a large number of such persons among the middle class society. They are the mainstay of humanity in this world.

THE STINGING MEMORY

The bee stings and pain lingers for a while
A memory stings and the pain lasts for a life

A bright life appeared and glittered for a decade
It showed promise to its creators and gave warmth of love
But suddenly God willed otherwise
And took it away to create darkness all around.

Should I take it as punishment or a lesson to learn?
I do not know
But the memory stings and torments
In moments of silence and loneliness

The knowledge of transitory life helps
To lighten the pain
But the sting remains to frequent the pain
And sour the rest of life

Should I blame my destiny or the destiny of the departed?
I do not know
But the torment is the same
And I writhe with pain the rest of my life

Why do relationships give pain when they are supposed to provide pleasure?

God only knows but men suffer for the ignorance
I shall ask when I go to meet the light
Why must darkness follow the light?

God is kind and the nature is kind
Then why must people have the pain?
Is it to tell us that pain must follow the pleasure
And life must end in death?

Is it to make us learn the lesson of life or believe in the Karma?
I do not know
For I only suffer in silence
And wait for the answer to come.

If love is to end in sorrow
And pleasure into pain
What gives me strength to survive and go through cycles of love and loss?
Perhaps a belief in the power unknown..

KEEPING VALUES

LIFE IN A METROPOLIS

Some people have the genius of turning a perfectly planned city into a slum. The principles involved are: unplanned addition in construction by defeating the municipal laws through bribery, occupation of pavement space by ignoring bylaws of construction, extending shops without permission, and considering government land as legitimately their own. Some people take pride in breaking laws, which are anyway not implemented with adequate seriousness. To compound the problem, the employees of implementing agencies are always in need of greasing their palms to keep them working. There is so much of friction in the system that it has become almost necessary to keep applying the grease in order to work the machine.

The persons who turn cities into slums are the ones for whom money is the religion. Their sole aim in life is to amass wealth by hook or by crook. They generally lack the sophistication of a cultured background; have poor education and an upbringing devoid of manners and sensibility. They are generally drunk with the power of wealth and connections, based on sycophancy and bribery. Their arrogance towards persons of education and decency is visible even to the unconcerned. They work on one principle; buy the powerful and enjoy life.

For those like me, who are used to walking as a mode of travel within the city rather than using a fuelled vehicle, the metropolis is not the place to live. I find the footpaths taken over by the vendors, and whatever is left used by shopkeepers as extension to their shops. If in a place less crowded, or in the suburban area, one finds any free footpath, it is invariably either broken or muddy. Coming from a small city, the metropolis looks like a zoo. People from all parts of the country with different traditions, different cultures and different habits, collect and make a living. There are posh areas and slums of abject poverty. The middle class grinds their days between the two extremes. There is no bonhomie of smaller cities. People look grim and tense. A look of worry seems to spread everywhere. The vendors are impolite and the shopkeepers react to persons of different status differently. Persons have no time to waste in idle pursuits like introduction and small talk. If you ask the way from a person who is in a hurry, he will give a dirty look and move away. Nobody has any time for anybody else. Everybody seems to be pre-occupied with his own problems.

If you have lived in a small city for some time, you develop some friendship with neighbors. But it is not so in a metropolis. Here people live in pigeonholes they call as apartments or flats. They spend all their money and attention in buying a new car and that gives them a status symbol. Their talk is mainly devoted to moneymaking; the newer and newer modes of partying, fashion and stock holdings. Even if the weather is kind, they sit in their air conditioned cars while idling; a totally wasteful mode of living.

Why do people reject the open-air environment of small cities and congregate in small holes in a metropolis? The answer is obvious. It is the lure of money that draws them to this congested environment where people feed on people. In modern age, the meaning of the 'quality of life' is skewed. The metropolitan people like less oxygen and more money.

FINDING A TRUE FRIEND

It is rather difficult to find a true friend in this self-oriented world of human activity. A true friend is one who comes to help in times of difficulty and does not expect anything in return. He advises correctly without any self-interest and always has the friend's interest at heart. It is wrong to say that there are no such persons existing today. But they are far and few to find in our daily life. Only some fortunate ones have them. They are a gift of nature.

Even among blood relations, one cannot expect really selfless persons to help, for they too expect the favor to be returned. A true friend is a person of spiritual orientation, for he believes in the universal values of life and acts on them as a part of duty. He is kind, loving and compassionate, and tolerant of others' faults. He cannot think of cheating those who put faith in him. He is a believer in the inherent capacity of man to understand others and acts accordingly. He relishes the success of others and is not jealous of them. His belief in the goodness of man is unshakeable. His heart is pure and his actions are transparent. Scheming, conniving and manipulating for self-advantage are anathema to him.

Such simple and idealist behavior is characteristic of a saintly person who has nothing but the interest of others at heart. He wants to see persons around him flourishing even at his own cost. Do we have such persons in this world? Yes, but they are a few dispersed in millions of selfish ones. They are elevated souls that come to lift others to their heights of selfless behavior.

CONTENTMENT

Thank God for what you have
And grumble not for what you don't
Contentment is a jewel that very few possess.

Spring of satisfaction should flow from heart and not from head
Grace comes from above and not from below
Embrace what He showers and be grateful
He knows what you deserve and is good for you

You can do only what you can
He has plans to do good to you
Despair not, for He knows all

IN GRATITUDE TO NATURE

In the fast paced life of modern age, it takes some effort to find time to think of God. In the olden days, people had enough spare time to reflect on life and think about the direction their life was taking on. These days, especially in big cities, it takes ten to twelve hours a day to earn enough to keep life going. People start early and come back late from work, a major part of time spent in going to and coming from the place of work. By the time they are back to their residence, they have no energy left to think of any thing worthwhile. It is too much to think of spiritual aspects of life from these tired workers. In addition there are domestic problems to be sorted out. No wonder we find most people in big cities looking harassed and sickly. Where is the time for them to appreciate nature and learn from it?

It is only the lucky ones in smaller towns and modernized villages who can appreciate the changes the seasons bring to the plants and trees; the buds opening themselves in smile, the shivering of trees in wintry breeze, the trees shedding their old garments of leaves, the rain drenching everything under the sun, the clouds joining together to form a uniform canvas of gray, the scorching summer with hot gusts of wind burning the earth under the feet, and the shooting of new leaves in the spring when the whole garden puts on a multicolored look of flowers and greens of different hues.

Watching the seasons, sadly missed by the city dweller, is an experience that delights the soul and lifts our mood away from the mundane problems. The experience makes our heads bow to the creator in gratitude. You then forget the sufferings of cold and heat and wait for the fruits of nature that delight you. Those who fail to feel obliged to nature and its master never really appreciate the good aspect of life and remember only the sufferings. They crib and grumble for what they haven't got rather than appreciate what they have. They are the ungrateful souls who have to come again and again on this earth to learn the lesson of life.

WHEN NOTHING SUCCEEDS, SURRENDER

When your anger does not produce result,
Try the language of tolerance.

When your threats and coercion fail,
Try the language of love

When enemy is defiant of your power,
Try the language of compassion

When your weapons of destruction are of no avail
Try the language of cooperation

When nothing succeeds,
Pray and surrender to the Master

THE CHANGING VALUES

The idealist picture of a saintly person is becoming blurred in practical world of today. Cheating, manipulating and cunning are gaining ground to over ride simplicity, frankness and straightforward dealings. People in increasingly large numbers are running to wealth and status. They have no time to reflect, spiritualize or think of humanist values for survival and progress. The spiritual person is losing ground to the greedy and the consumerist. The advice of the saner elements to become loving and kind is falling on deaf ears. There is a general downslide of spiritual values, spiritual teaching and ethical values in trade and commerce. The hope of revival of the spiritual standards is receding. The optimism about revival of moral way of life is vanishing and vulgarity in speech and action is receiving general consent. The society is beginning to accept corruption and bribery as an accepted way of life. We no longer dislike unethical ways of making money. Power and wealth are becoming the new gods.

The only hope for mankind is possibly the people will tire out with money and power and will start seeking solace in spiritual advice. Hopefully, the adverse effects of running after wealth and power will increase the stress levels sufficiently that people will start slowing down on account of a necessity to survive in good health and happiness. They may ultimately discover that happiness lies in silent pursuit of spirituality and not running the rat race.

Fashions change, morals change, and social convictions change too. Ideas about good and bad change with time as history of social change testifies. Human mind is restless. It seeks new thoughts all the time. There is inherent urge to experiment with the new and shed the old.

The spirit of change is inherent in nature. This provides the promise of saving the world from chaos and decline. Without this spirit of change in nature, the evolution of man would not have been possible. Evolution and revolution are embedded in the continuity of human history.

The intellect has its own role in exploration and continuous change. One wants to seek out something that one does not have. It gives rise to invention and discovery. Technologies develop with time and change the way people live. With or without belief, the social structures change. It is best to move with the times and accept change rather than delay with obsolete and obstinate views resisting change.

Decline is as much a part of the system as the advancement. The cyclic pattern of nature is accepted in Vedic system of thought. The rise and fall of civilizations is known to take place with regularity in the history of mankind. Nations that ruled the world are known to reduce to insignificance and suffering millions are raised to heights of prosperity. There is no point in cribbing about decline or change of ways. The inevitable will happen. It is best to accept it with grace and go along living in the best way you can.

The nature should take you towards the Reality and not draw you away from it

In order that God within meets the God in temple, close your eyes and think of the whole

THE POPULOUS STATE

I live in a country that has the distinction of having a population only second to the highest. There are people everywhere, be it the railway platform, the bank, the milk booth, the enquiry window, the shop in a mall or the stationery shop. There is a queue everywhere whenever you have to do any odd job. Even for paying bills you have to stand in a long line of human beings, much like the ants moving in a straight line. The most precious commodity is to find a lonely place if you are in a mood to reflect. The houses have shrunk in carpet area because there are too many people to accommodate in a small place. It is a constant struggle for existence as a private person. To get a room exclusively for you is a luxury that only the upper middle class can afford. For most people of middle-income group, finding a flat of reasonable size is like finding a goldmine that no body has visited. In the peak hours of work, it is next to impossible to stand even six inches away from another person. The mean free path is reduced to a few steps. One would expect the situation to be better in a park in the morning or evening. But alas, there too, the average density of walkers and strollers is high enough to deter the weak hearted. The probability of collision increases as the girth diameter is increased with sedentary life style.

According to a political opinion, a large population is an asset to a country. But it is true only if the majority is young, talented, skilled, and most important, a disciplined lot. It is a liability if the major part is illiterate, unskilled and has scant respect for law. I find it quite irritating when the persons standing in the queue suddenly decide to break it as soon as the window is opened. Without discipline no nation is worth its salt. To claim preference on the basis of wealth, status or political power is downright insulting to others. Even if the state has a high GDP, an arsenal of deadly weapons and a large force to implement laws, the country hardly deserves respect if its citizens have no respect for law.

The law is best implemented when there is equality before law, equality not on paper but in implementation. The lawbreakers have to be dealt with strictness and judged irrespective of the status of the person. But unfortunately, where avenues for enrichment are few and unequal, there is always the tendency for greasing the palm to get what one wants. This unavoidably distorts the system and the have-nots suffer the most. Making more laws is in fructuous if the implementation is flawed.

In my view, that country deserves to be called poor in which the law enforcement structures are poor and discriminative. A disciplined nation will always rise sooner or later because the thinking of the majority is right. The availability of resources is only a secondary factor. Tendency to work hard in a collectively disciplined manner is the prime requirement. Everything comes next. History has shown the truth of this fact. I do not subscribe to the view that growth means wealth generation and discipline follows the growth of GDP. It is the inherent quality of man that makes a nation great. Mere slogans and preaching of the politicians are of no consequence in making a country great. It is the quality of leadership, both in intellect and self-discipline, which matters to the people.

THE FEELING OF INSECURITY

There is a feeling of insecurity in many spheres of life. There is financial insecurity, the fear of physical attack and robbery, the social insecurity, the insecurity of rejection and failure, the insecurity about survival and so on. If you come to think of it, the fundamental insecurity is that of survival. If by some means you can overcome the fear of death, most feelings of insecurity will vanish. Financial security and social security are also about survival.

Feeling of security comes when you are assured that no harm is likely to come to you because of the wealth and power you enjoy, except the unforeseen circumstances of natural disasters. All fears can however be overcome once you are convinced that this life is not the only life you live. The idea of rebirth plays a significant part in alleviating the fear of death. If you know that after death you are going to live, either in spirit or in another body, you become free of the fear of losing this life.

One would expect safety in a large gathering of likeminded people. But in practice this is not so. One feels lonelier in a crowd and less sure of oneself if the crowd is of diverse cultures with minority phobia. Crowding together of minorities, building walls against other cultures and creating boundaries with other cities and countries are all manifestations of the feeling of insecurity. Possession of military strength by countries tries to create a feeling of security among the civil population, but this hardly succeeds in its purpose because there is all the time fear of matching strength by the enemies. People of neighboring countries, which are always at loggerheads, can hardly feel safe and secure because there is continuous fear of attack by the neighbor.

The feeling of insecurity at individual level can be removed by the spiritual assurance of after life since it provides a continuity that is not disturbed by the severance of this life. Sages have dwelt at length on the subject of eternity for the simple reason that all are afraid of death. Removing this fear is a great service to humanity. Though most religions of earlier days had this concept of rebirth incorporated in their religious beliefs, some religions later dropped it for reasons extraneous to the concept. Eastern religions however still persist with this, with the obvious advantage of providing psychological advantage of removing the fear of death.

The desire to last forever is reflected in the famous saying of the Upanishad
(O Lord)
Take me from darkness to light,
From ignorance to knowledge
And from death to eternity

SPIRITUAL GROWTH

IT IS A MATTER OF HEAD AND HEART

The often talked about topic of science and spirituality is really a matter of head and heart. Science is a subject that indulges in analysis, argument and evidence in the phenomenal world to prove a point intellectually. Spirituality is an experience of universal love that is beyond reasoning and argument.

The difference in reason and emotion is characteristic of the difference in head and heart. To search one in the other is a futile exercise that leads nowhere. To reason out God and to obtain the evidence of God are perhaps taken care of in the domain of science and philosophy that involves the brain. But to experience God is a matter of heart. Without universal love and compassion, the experience of God is a near impossibility. If you do not believe in the universality of life and have no respect for it, you cannot reach anywhere near God. The Upanishads explain it beautifully while dealing with emotion and intellect.

If you try to experience God through intellect, you are wasting time. The ladder of intellect has to be thrown out once you have reached the lowest level of intuitive existence. You are then not depending on your intellect but on the love and grace of God. Intellect is meant to serve the purpose of worldly interaction; gathering phenomenological knowledge, analyzing it and using it for comfortable living through technological development. It is not for entering the domains that are beyond the limits of space and time. For that you have to depend on the power of universal love, which is a force that spans the whole existence, visible and invisible, a force that transcends space, time, and duality.

It is not necessary that you add to the knowledge base of the world in a significant way
It is important that you put a drop in the ocean of knowledge.

It is not imperative to be a spiritual recluse
It is necessary that you improve your interaction with the creation of God

It is not necessary that your good actions are visible to the world
It is important that you help an unknown entity in all seriousness

It is not important that you become the wealthiest or the most powerful
It is necessary that you develop a sense of humility, kindness and compassion

It is not necessary that you advertise your goodness and greatness
It is important that your actions are transparent to the One who matters

It is not necessary to perform cleansing rituals
It is important that you clean your thoughts

TO AN UNHAPPY FRIEND

We seek happiness through wealth, power and position
Not knowing, happiness is neither for sale, nor can be forced or snatched.

A state of mind that happiness is,
It is through contentment, giving and sharing
We barter it with others

In God's trust and fellow feeling
We generate a happy environment
In selfless love we receive satisfaction
In ego we become discontented
And march to dominate others
In politics, business and technology

Spirituality is not a thing of the other world.
It is a means to the goal of joyous happiness
See God in every one and you know the truth
The truth that ennobles our life
The truth that is eternally within us
But remains dormant through ignorance and deceit

Look within and find happiness
It lies not outside
Help others and find happiness
Love for others is divine

Smile with the flower and the world will smile with you
Blame the world for unhappiness and you will weep alone

Conquer the world with sword and you spread the fear
Conquer the hearts with love and you earn respect

God will not force anything against your will
For he has given you the freewill to act
Act right and be happy, for it is your right
Act wrong and be unhappy, blame not your destiny

CLEANING OF THE INNER BEING

We are all aware of the need to clean physically; the body, the house, the office and the living environment of cities. It is done not once but periodically because dirt and dust accumulate with time. Also, unclean surroundings spread disease and degradation. But we rarely think of cleaning the inner being and the subconscious. The unclean minds too spread disease in the mental environment, both personal and social. This too needs periodic cleaning through spiritual practices prescribed in different religious streams. The rituals associated with the religious festivals are meant to serve this very purpose, though in practice we often forget the real intention and resort to mere outward actions.

Cleaning of the inner being is much more difficult than physical cleaning. The need to physical cleaning is apparent to us because the results of not doing this are immediately known to us in our daily experiences. We fall sick if we do not clean our body. The epidemics spread if we keep our environment dirty. But if one or more persons behave badly, we tend to ignore them and go on with our work putting the blame on education system or the lack of civic sense. We take no measures to reflect and clean our thoughts on a regular basis. Only when the mental stress becomes too high on us, we think of slowing down and correct our ways of working. If somebody advises to resort to spiritual methods, we either ignore him or laugh it off as an unnecessary deviation from the normal way of life. We find excuses in science or rationality and consider spirituality as the escapist way of life.

Only in the last quarter of a century, the scientists have begun appreciating the importance of cleaning the mind, because we have established the relationship of mind with matter scientifically. We know the mind matter relation in running our biological system, the effect of thought on autonomic system and so on. We now treat mind body complex as one unit and not separate as we did earlier. The fast paced life of big cities has forced this information to become a part of our medical knowledge. Psychology and psychiatry have attained as much importance as the treatment procedures of medicine and surgery. Meditation is now a tool to reckon with in the treatment of psychosomatic diseases.

What do we mean by cleaning of the inner being that spiritual people talk of? It is the right thinking, right actions and right living. It means appreciating the universalism as a desired way of life. We need to appreciate and act accordingly in the interest of society and not for self-alone. For this we need to know our true self. We must know that we are integral to the social structure and part of the universal whole. If we destroy any part of it in self-interest, we cause damage to ourselves. We are not an independent entity but a part of the whole. We cannot usurp others' rights because ultimately it will back fire on us. If we hate others or become angry with somebody, it has a direct effect on our body as well. If in our greed we consume more than what is genuinely required for our sustenance, we degrade the environment and put our own survival at stake.

Love others and you will be loved. If you snatch from others, your own security will be jeopardized.

Physical cleaning and spiritual cleaning must go hand in hand. In the modern age of complex living, it is not only desirable but a must for future survival.

THE DARKNESS WITHIN

It is common in spiritual circles that a clear and clean heart is better than outward religiosity and show of virtuosity. There is an anecdote in this connection that illustrates the point.

There was a rich businessman who was known in his community as a very religious person. He went to temple regularly and spent considerable time in worship of idols. On every religious function he occupied the place of pride and importance. He donated to the religious cause liberally and was known to go for listening to every discourse that took place in the temple. He had also hired a servant to do the various chores in his household. Though he paid liberally to him for his services, he often scolded him for minor faults and thought that it was his birthright to treat him the way he liked because after all he was dependent on him. He never gave him leave to go and meet his relatives and enjoy with his family. Whenever there was any function in the family, he engaged him from morning to evening without a moment of rest. The servant on his part accepted this hardship as his destiny and never complained. He carried out his task with utmost honesty and sincerity to the best of his capability.

One day, he looked puzzled in the morning and went to his master and said, ' Sir, last night I had a dream in which your lord in the temple appeared to me and said that he was pleased with my work and wanted to reward me. But I told him that I was ok with my master and did not need any thing except His blessings.' He then asked his master if he needed any thing so that if He appeared again, he could ask that from Him. This annoyed his master immensely. The master felt angry about this attitude of his God. He thought, ' I do so much service to Him but he ignored me and talked to my servant who is dependent on my kindness. How could God be so indifferent to my offerings and my prayers and be kind to the servant who has nothing to give to him and never even goes to the temple. It only proves that God is partial to his people.' However, he did not express his feelings to any body and told his servant that next time if He appears then tell him why He is not talking to me. When He comes in my dream, I will ask Him what I want from Him.

The next day, the servant again came to his master and said, ' Sir, I asked last night what you told me and He has replied that since I am doing my duty without any expectation, he feels obliged to favor me. As regards yourself, He said that you bring business in all your dealings and have no regard for the feelings of people. Therefore He does not accept your favors and offerings and does not want to give any thing more than you already have.' This completely floored his master and he got the message that God does not like bargaining. If you have to win Him, you have to have a kind and just nature and treat every body equal with no strings attached. He does not distinguish between master and servant because both are His children. He is impartial to all and partial to none but to win his favor you have to give up partiality first. Due to our negativity in mind, we have created a darkness within us that shrouds the light of the spirit that resides in us. Unless we remove this darkness by cleaning our heart, we cannot hope to see His brilliance within us. It does not matter what status in life we possess. No body is big enough to demand from God his favor or grace. It is He who decides what we deserve.

THE RISE OF CONSCIOUSNESS

We are conscious of our surroundings through our senses. This sense consciousness increases with our knowledge of external world as we grow and learn through books and experiences. We learn that we are living on a planet that is part of a solar system, which again is a part of the Milky Way galaxy. Our galaxy is again one of the many such galaxies that form the universe. This knowledge of our physical existence is achieved through our interaction with outside environment with the use of instrumentation in conjunction with our senses. Does it make us more conscious of our existence? To some extent yes. But this does not tell us any thing about our other planes of existence, the intuitive planes and the mental states of realizing our true identity.

Science may tell us that we are in fact not the matter that we appear to be but in the ultimate analysis we are just packets of energy floating in vacuum. This takes us to another level of consciousness where every thing is seen in its true form of just energy. Spiritually conscious persons however, tell us that this is not the whole story. They say that our true nature, as that of other material beings, is the spirit that pervades universally as pure consciousness. The pure consciousness is the knowledge of just being, a state of blissful existence that is eternal and infinite.

The rise in consciousness in spiritual sense is the knowledge of our true nature of just being. It is neither the body, nor the mind, nor even the intellect. It is a state that is different from our three states of existence; wakefulness, dream and deep sleep. It is the fourth state of existence of thoughtless existence where physicality turns into divinity. In the divine state, we are intuitively knowledgeable, free from the bounds of space and time. It is a state of pure existence, free and limitless. Birth and death and cycles of nature have no relevance to it. It is free from time, events and change, which are characteristic of nature. It is the cause of nature and not the effect of it. It is self-luminous and ever present. This state is experienced not through senses but intuitively through meditative practices.

According to Aurobindo, the consciousness is dormant in the nonliving matter but continually rises in living matter to higher levels in order to reach the ultimate state of pure consciousness. It is the ultimate fate of all levels of consciousness to reach the divine state of just being. This play of consciousness is the divine Leela, or the play of nature that goes on eternally. We also know from science that energy only changes form. It never dies out. Conservation of energy is a fundamental principle of our scientific knowledge. All this shows that we are eternal in our true nature. The death is a temporary transitional stage of our existence. In the true sense we never die. It is just a change in material form, to a spiritual existence in a different plane of existence. If we know this for sure, there is no ground for fear of death. This gives us freedom in true sense.

KEEPING COOL IN THE ROUGH AND TUMBLE OF LIFE

Most of us get annoyed and lose our cool when things go wrong. It is a natural reaction that we learn from our parents, teachers and acquaintances in similar situations. Though we are taught in school to keep our cool, it is rarely that we can put this advice into practice. There is something wrong with the teaching that advises us to remain cool. It is the lack of example that the teachers themselves present to us in difficult situations. Their teachings and practices do not go together. The reason lies in the behavioral practices we see day in and day out in our lifetime, from childhood to adolescence, which is the formative part of our life.

Why do we get angry when our desires are not fulfilled? It is out of sheer helplessness that confronts us. There are factors that are beyond pour reach that control the situation. Even though all of us go through rough patches, this is no consolation to us. We want all of our desires to be fulfilled, even though we know it is not possible because there is no end to desire and we are not the only persons important enough in this world. Nature has its own way of teaching us the facts of existence. We get what we deserve, no more and no less. What we deserve comes from our actions, and not as favor or reproof.

The ability to remain calm in adversity comes from understanding and tolerance for others; the understanding of others needs, their aspirations and the knowledge that others too have desires. One's individuality should be balanced against the universality of nature. The world is not made for you alone. It is the relationship between peoples that runs this world. The desires of all have to be met within the resources of this world. An attitude of tolerance is necessary because there are people who have better qualities and higher capacity than yours.

The best way to develop a calm and cool temperament is to understand that every one is equal in the eyes of God and that God resides in all in equal measure. We are all children of same God and we have to share the resources of nature with a sense of equality and brotherhood. No one has a better claim just because one is more intelligent or more powerful or wealthier. Power, and wealth are transitory acquisitions and intellect is given to interact with the outside world. No one has the birthright to dominate over others based on acquired possessions. As human beings all are born equal in the eyes of God. All inequalities are man made based on self-interest and communal considerations.

Keeping cool under provocation should not be seen as a sign of weakness since it requires quite a bit of self-control to do so. One needs to develop self-control as a prerequisite to avoid confrontation. It is very easy to fly in rage and commit blunders, but it requires a great maturity and a sense of balance to remain quite under unfavorable circumstances. It is not only necessary to avoid conflict in personal life but also in matters of social and political conflicts. The world would be a much better place if spiritual advice were adhered to in maintaining calm in our life and in the life of others. We need more saints in this world than warmongers. Our prayers should be for the peace and stability of society than for the power and wealth of individual centers of domination. May God hive us wisdom to bring heaven on earth rather than looking above for it.

EMOTIONAL DISCIPLINE

Emotions form an integral part of our personality. A word, an event or even a gesture can trigger emotional response in us. While some can control their emotional response, there are others who flare up immediately in positive or negative manner depending upon the nature of trigger. Wise persons tell us to be objective in responding to emotional inputs so that we conserve our energy for better purposes. Some of the emotions are volatile, some the simmering kind while some are disturbing and destroying. Among the emotions of negative kind are anger, hatred, jealousy, pride and greed. Emotions of love, compassion, care and contentment produce a positive effect.

Every one has a touch of emotions of both positive and negative type, though some have predominance of one over the other. If there were no emotion of love and care in a mother, the offspring would not survive. If there were no emotion of aggression in predators, they would probably die of hunger. Man has combined the cunning with intellect to overpower other species. The frequency of responding to emotion is another factor that governs the personality of an individual. For some it becomes a habit to repeatedly offend others out of jealousy or self-interest.

In order to be spiritually wise, it is necessary to rise above negative emotions and be loving, compassionate, tolerant and forgiving. Why is this discipline necessary? It is for the simple reason that negative emotions degrade a person physically and mentally. Anger causes stress that may last long if it is mixed with hatred. Greed may make a person undesirable from the point of social stability. Pride may cause a sense of domination; a negative trait as far as spiritual health is concerned. All these negative qualities may lead to a stressful situation both for the individual as well as the society at large. If not checked in time, they turn into habits that harm the growth of a happy life. Spiritual training emphasizes that removing negative traits is the prerequisite to spiritual growth.

Violence is a direct result of anger and hatred. In religion, intolerance of others views and way of life results in fanaticism and strife within social structures. Most problems of social discord arise because we are not willing to accept others way of life. We want others to follow our traditions, our customs and our rituals. This is extended to such ludicrous dimensions that we resort to terrorism and violent ways to make others succumb to you. But for the pleadings and saner advice from the philosophers and secular leadership, the human race would have behaved like wild animals. Instead of understanding the religious views in proper context, we make our own interpretations to suit our purpose. We think that our religion is the best and any deviation from its underlying principles is blasphemy. We criticize poets, philosophers and writers of satire as enemies of faith.

Proper discipline of emotions is necessary for every society that wants to found itself on reason and rationality. Tolerance of conflicting views shows a maturity level that is right for a stable and prosperous nation state. Evolution is to be not only in biological sense but in social sense as well. Strong bodies must go hand in hand with mature minds.

THE INEVITABILITY OF SPIRITUAL GROWTH

The spiritualists are optimists. According to them, it is the destiny of man to ultimately realize the self. Some may do it early with spiritual practices while the rest will leave it to their fate, even though it may take many births. But the ascent to pure consciousness is inevitable. It may be evaded for a time but in the end all must come to it. It is just that some who are spiritually conscious use extra effort to reach it early while the others move slowly to evolve with nature to higher consciousness. Every man has the qualities that are required for his evolution towards the enlightenment.

Saints and mystics are not special human beings. What one man possesses the other man has it too in him. The spiritually oriented use their god-given faculties with extra effort to reach the spiritual goal while others ignore theses faculties and chase the worldly dreams. Consciously or unconsciously we are all moving towards the same goal, some fast and some slowly. In this movement some seek intellectual understanding; others go for moral uplift and still others for mystical experiences. Every one attains a level that motivates him to go further at his own speed of self-development. Those who are asleep, half awakened or more awakened than others are all moving to the same goal at their own pace of awakening, willingly or unwillingly. They are consciously or unconsciously inspired by the same supreme power and take part in His scheme of things.

It is wrong to say that mystic's knowledge and experience is of no concern to the ordinary person. Spiritual knowledge is of concern to all. It concerns their happiness and freedom. Every common man is unknowingly moving towards spiritual goal by improving the conduct and sticking to universal values of existence. The spiritual awareness of a common man lies latent in him. One only needs to ignite his spirit and awaken his potential to reach the goal. Even a criminal mind is as much equipped for spiritual growth as the devotee of God. It is only a question of triggering the mechanism in him to shift his focus to spirituality. He has the same body-mind-intellect as any other person.

Bhagwadgita says there is hope for all, sinners and seekers alike. The whole humanity in a way is slowly moving to the spiritual goal, which is the aim of existence. Some are doing faster than others. But that is not a cause for concern. It is also true that of all those who start the journey only a few reach the destination. But that is only because a few carry the interest or the desire to succeed till the end. Also, not all are looking for the Truth. Small successes on the way carry most of the starters away. Some are happy to get cured while some are satisfied with psychic powers. Only a few keep moving in the search for truth. In terms of numbers, seekers of truth are far less than the seekers of personal help in body and mind. The reason for this disparity in numbers is that not many are willing to crush their ego. It is a path of discipline and sustained effort. Most men and women are happy to live in body, mind and intellect. Only a few opt to go forward and widen their consciousness.

GOD'S PRESENCE

I have often wondered why is it that most people cannot visualize the presence of God in every thing when the very nature of God is such that it should be the easiest thing to do so. I think the reason is that most people fail to realize the true nature of God. They perceive Him to be either a person, or an unknowable being, that is beyond the capacity of our senses. The latter is understood in the sense that we cannot see God with our eyes nor hear Him with our ears. But then we know from science that creative energy is omnipresent in the universe; it should obviously follow that God, the creative entity, must be present everywhere including the human beings. To see the energy, one can only see the effect of it. But to experience it intuitively in nature, one must have the right spiritual sense.

Enlightenment, God-realization, God –consciousness are synonymous terms that describe the psychic stage when we see God present in every particle of the universe. Our own presence in this state of realization becomes one with that of God where the seer, the seen and the process of seeing all merge into one whole. The nature is then seen as a manifestation of God/energy.

The faculties of thought, speech and action are because of this energy's presence within us. There is very little to distinguish between bodies before one second of death and one second after death. It is His presence that makes the difference, so say the mystics.

BEAUTY AND BLISS

After the rain, a gust of wind came
And the water drops fell from the leaves of plants and trees
When they fell on the tender shoots
They displayed a beauty none could ignore

The drops then danced on the earth
And enriched the soil with their energy
Who could be ignorant of the power behind the drops
That beckons us to join the bliss of creative energy

Even if God did not exist
I will join the play of nature
And rejoice with it

The pleasure is enjoyed with heart and not head
The intellect analyses the phenomena
And spoils the fun

The power behind nature exists
And combines beauty with bliss.

THE WAY PEOPLE LIVE

THE ROAD TO HILLS

It was a long ride on a road that never seemed to end. The rough ride made the body ache. The road went straight like a stretched rope and was known to end in rising mountains. In the mountains it transformed in to a twisted rope much like the movement of a snake. When our patience seemed to give way, I saw the rising mountains, which promised a more difficult ride. I was thinking of a comfortable stay in the hills, a thought that kept me going even on a difficult journey like this. Thinking of the prospect that lay ahead, I decided to have a break for a while.

On coming out of the vehicle, I sighted a small thatched roof on the side of the road. It housed a makeshift kind of room with water boiling in a kettle and some cheap sweets to serve as snacks. It was typical of a tea vending stall that adorn the highway roads for weary travelers who enjoy the hot cup of tea more than the snacks on offer. We too decided to have a seat and enjoy the environment with the refreshing cup of tea. Just to spend time in conversation, I asked the vendor how was life in the village and what was his main activity besides this tea stall. I thought there wouldn't be many customers for him to make a living only on this tea business. Perhaps he did it as a side business to make a few extra bucks.

The vendor was a middle-aged man of strong built, with a face that hid more emotions than it displayed.

He seemed to have a kind heart and a genuine concern for his customers. He enjoyed talking to his customers to make them at ease. While we were talking, I saw a small boy who stood nearby and looked unhappy for some reason. I interrupted my talk and asked the man what was wrong with that boy. He hesitated a moment and then said,' sir, his mother has left him in my charge and gone in the nearby jungle to collect wood to sell in the evening. She does not take him with her fearing that some harm may come to him if she does so. The jungle has some wild animals.' I was astonished to hear that and said,'but then is she not taking a chance with him remaining all alone here with no body to look after her?' The tea vendor told me that he had taken his responsibility unofficially and that his mother had confidence that he would be safe with him.

Soon we realized that we had finished our tea and it was time to start again as we had to travel some distance, and that too in hills where sun sets early. As we were about to move out of the shop, I saw that boy's mother come to him and the boy rushing to meet her. I found that the mother had a rustic beauty with good health and sharp features. Even though she had returned with a big bundle of wood for fuel, she radiated a confidence and a charm that was captivating. She then gave the wood to the vendor in return for money with which she bought some sweet for the boy. Her motherly affection was infectious. Nobody could ignore the bond that existed between the boy and his mother. In passing her, I asked, 'are you not afraid of leaving your child to the care of strangers?' She boldly replied,' sir, we poor people do not have much choice in the way we live. Call it our destiny or our Karma. But we have no grudge against anybody. We leave our lives in the care of Almighty, and He does not ditch us.' It was refreshing to know the philosophical attitude at her level of understanding. We said good-bye to the vendor and moved on.

In the hills, I had to cover a function in which the political figure of the region was to address a meeting as part of the contact program. The politician gave an enthusiastic picture of the region for the upliftment of women, particularly those who had no support from any quarter. He praised his own efforts to rehabilitate the women who had lost their husbands in the service of the nation. He further promised to launch big schemes for those who had to fend for their daily bread. To me it all looked hollow. But I was only doing my duty to convey his promises and achievements to people as elaborated by the worthy leader.

After the function I asked the local people for their reaction to the leader's speech. To my expectation, they all said that they had heard him umpteen times repeating these words, which they now knew by heart. I was rather disappointed at the state of affairs because I had seen the reality at the vendor's shop. Women like the one we had encountered at the vendors hut were probably not in the list of the leaders who day in and day out boasted of their upliftment programs.

After finishing our work in the hills, it was now time to move back. After the arduous journey of hills, we again stopped at the same tea vendor's shop for a hot cup of tea. The vendor was happy to see us again. Out of curiosity, I asked the vendor about the woman and child. He became very serious and signs of worry appeared on his face. With great effort he replied, 'the women did not return from the jungle last night. The boy has been crying all night. We fear the worst, as there is a talk of a tiger becoming man-eater. Some persons in the village have gone looking for the woman. But we are not very hopeful since the woman would never leave the child for such a long time. The boy is every thing for her and he is the only reason of her living in this world.'

After hearing this I could not drink my tea as something touched my heart so violently that I lost balance for a while. A heart-rending anger sprouted for the creator who enacted such scenes for poor souls who have no body to speak for them. Is it divine justice? I do not know. Certainly, good hardworking people deserve better. I was sad for the poor boy that had to face the loss of both parents at such a young age.

Before starting back, I asked the vendor, 'what will happen to the boy now?'

The vendor replied in mute tones, 'he will share my life and poverty equally'

I did not take tea for a month.

THE BUS RIDE

It was an old rickety bus, creaking along the dusty path, making others on the road know its presence with the noise and polluting smoke. It was a bus that connected a few villages with the city. It was packed to its capacity and overflowing with luggage and a few passengers that staked their life for the pleasure of riding over it. Its fitness certificate must have been signed in sleep or the grease must have smoothened the palm of the inspecting officer. The passengers had the luggage that took more space than the seats on which they sat. A loud music of old songs was blaring to the limit of the ears. The driver, sitting on the steering, was happily tuned to the music. Even though it was difficult to have a conversation in this loud music, some passengers did seem to talk and share their daily experiences. The seats were meant to give you a cushioning effect but with use they had become hard as wood. The potholes on the road, of the size of a football, added to the discomfort, which the passengers bought. The dirt, the heat and the smell of the sweat completed the picture of journey.

I was a passenger not by choice but by necessity. I was going to see a friend of mine who was visiting his parents in the village. To ease the discomfort of the bus journey, I thought of picking up some conversation with a co-passenger who seemed to be agreeable to talk. I asked him, 'how often do you travel in this bus because you seem to be quite unaffected by this uncomfortable journey.' He gave me a smile and said, ' in fact I travel quite frequently because my business is to buy cloth from the city and sell it to the villagers. I have a family to feed and this is my living.' But this is a very difficult way of earning, I thought. I thanked God for sparing me this vocation because if I was in his position I would have broken down in no time.

To continue the conversation, I asked him whether this mode of living was thrust on him or he did it by choice. He took some time before he spoke again. He said, ' I consider every work as the work of God. I do it because I have been put in these circumstances by my destiny. I have no grudge against any body. All work to me is worship of God. This world is of God. I am His creation, and I do what is provided to me by the prevailing conditions. I am neither happy nor unhappy. It is as good a work as any. I do service to the poor peasants who have no means to go to city and make purchases. I do not charge them more than what I need for my family's needs. It is an arrangement that suits me as much as it does to the buyers. Why should I feel bad about it? After all these farmers are also traveling in the same mode as I am doing. Feeling uncomfortable is a state of mind, which I control with my thinking. The whole world cannot travel in luxury. Every body cannot be a millionaire. There are people who have to compromise their status with their resources. I do not wish to offend you, but once a while one must feel the pain of poor people. The world is not meant for display of wealth and comfort. It is meant to do the bidding of God, and that is what I do.'

I was rather stunned by this reply because I expected him to agree with me about the discomfort and consequent suffering to make a living. I expected him to seek sympathy. But he completely floored me with his frank reply and the level of his spiritual thought. Many people, learned and urbane, talk about the advice of Bhagwadgita but hardly put that advice in practice. Here was a person who personified the very essence of the Gita.

THE TEMPLE ON THE HILL

I was on vacation and so was the family. We had decided on a hill journey to a well-known town that was famous for its temple. When we started from our base camp, the hotel, for the temple, it was quite foggy and the road had a visibility of only a few feet. We felt a little apprehensive, because the hill journey was quite tortuous and winding all the way. We were however assured by the driver that it will be all right since the fog does not stay for long. He was proved right soon, for the fog lifted after fifteen minutes and we moved with confidence for the rest of the journey.

It was refreshing to enjoy the greenery all around on the slopes of the hills. Every turn however, presented a challenge to the driver. The narrow hill roads, un-paved at places, are quite frightening to the inexperienced drivers like me. I was therefore not at ease till we reached the temple of our destination. It was perched at the top of the hill, and gave the look of an unattended place, for not many people seemed to have visited before us. But on the tourist map it occupied a place of prominence. It was an old temple of Siva with the simplicity that goes with such temples.

The ascent to the hill was steep and took some effort to reach the top. But once you reached there the scene all around was so captivating that you did not feel like coming to ground. It was all green and hilly. There were a few huts here and there to remind you of your human existence. Below the temple there were a few thatched shops, which catered to the daily needs of the residents. By looking down from above, it gave you the feeling as if you were looking down on the mundane existence from the divine height.

After enjoying the heavenly sight for some time, we descended from the temple to the residence of the priest. It appeared strange that a person could live at such a lonely place all alone in this jungle for years without feeling tired of loneliness. I therefore asked him how he felt living there alone without any assistance. He told me it was no problem to him as he enjoyed the company of trees and the temple deity. Still unconvinced, I said that surely he must have been feeling the absence of his dear ones that he possibly left behind to choose this life. He said that the true love is not of relations but that of the one who has created all. It is the love of the creator that he sought and it is in his memory that he spends most of his time. Faith and love of God are tremendous forces that can keep a person alive in all loneliness. Further, he had come there with a mission. It was to meditate and realize himself of the truth of his existence. He was so engrossed in the success of his mission that he had no time to think of questions like the one I posed. It was a signal for me to grow up and stop asking silly questions from a saintly person.

I realized then that there are persons in this world whose objective in life can be quite different from the normal routine of mere existence. It is only such persons who show light to those who crib and groan under the weight of mundane existence that circles round bread, clothing and shelter. If you run after pleasure and comfort, they recede from you and tease you to tears. But if you neglect them for a higher purpose they become insignificant for you and cannot attract your attention. I came back to my place certainly a wiser person.

THE ROPE WAY

The addition of a ropeway on tourist spots located on top of hills serves as an additional attraction for those who come from plains in summer to enjoy the heights of mountains. I am one of those who are attracted to mountains in the summer season. It is almost a ritual with me. On one such occasion when I was enjoying the rush of people around a ropeway, I happened to see a boy in his adolescence trying to attract tourists to the ropeway ride. He was obviously engaged by the contractor to do this service in exchange for some remuneration. The expression on the face of the boy was of a reluctance to do such a job. He was obviously forced by circumstances of his family to do this menial work. I, therefore, asked him what made him do this work. He rather hesitatingly answered that he was doing this to supplement the income of his family. To know more about his circumstances, I further asked, 'don't you have your father to bring enough money to the family?' This made the boy put on a sullen face and rather reluctantly he answered, ' I do have my father who is a casual laborer. But he does not earn enough to make both of us eat two meals a day and also pay for my school fee. I have therefore to do odd jobs to earn something extra to pay for my fees and also buy occasionally something special to eat. The situation was different when my mother was alive. She was then doing the job of supplementing father's income. But after she died this responsibility fell on me. What looks strange to you people is in fact quite normal to us poor people.'

Hearing him, I could not but become concerned with his plight. I wondered how many people have to live like this in this free country of ours on which we pride. Child labor is a matter of intense discussion among the politicians and all of them swear by the absence of it in this country. But the ground situation is different as you can always see poor children engaged in supplementing the family income one way or the other. Some admit it and some don't. On paper, the family does not need the dole. But the practical reality forces the family to depend on every member to contribute to the family kitty. I just felt sorry for the boy and left the scene.

Next year I returned to find the boy selling tidbits instead of working for the contractor. I asked him what happened to his earlier job. Recognizing me, he became friendly and replied, 'sahib, the contractor fired me for not attracting enough tourists and besides I had to earn more since my father became weak and could not lift as much baggage as he used to do earlier. I therefore chose to do this business on the side. Even though it takes more time, it is worth the effort since I need more money. I asked him whether he believed in God or fate. He said, ' sir these things are for the older people who have more time to think of such things. As far as I am concerned, I believe He is everywhere and so must know my situation. If He knows it and does not help, why should I worry about Him? I, in fact have very little time left to myself to think of such things. My mother believed in Him but he took her away. Now both my father and I do not bother Him with our condition. Let Him take care of the rich and the influential that offer him costly gifts and sweets.' There was obviously some tinge of bitterness in his belief in Him. He was indeed justified to hold it so. I left him to his earning engagement and moved away to other attractions that had been added that year for the tourists.

I bade him good luck in his new venture and passed on to new attractions introduced that year for the tourists.

After another year, I returned with a friend and looked for the boy. I was interested to know how he was doing in his small business. But when I reached the site of the ropeway, much to my surprise, I did not find him there. I asked one or two boys who were similarly engaged, but they did not know him. I was about to return disappointed when an old man came to me and said. ' Are you looking for that boy whom you talked to last year?' When I said yes, he told me that the boy had left this place and was now working as a full-fledged coolie at the bus station. I must admit that I was rather surprised because the boy was interested in studies and he worked only part time to help his father.

To know the real reason for his shift to new mode of working, I asked my friend to accompany me to the bus station. I was curious to know why he had left his studies. When I went there, the boy immediately recognized me and smilingly asked how I was doing. I in turn asked him the same question and told him that I was eager to know his reasons for leaving the studies. He kept his smile on and said, 'sahib, my father died six months back due to over work. I had no means to live the life of a student since part time working was not giving me enough to sustain myself. Moreover, the competition at that place had increased due to other part timers joining the same occupation. I had therefore, no alternative but to become a full time earner. Sir, the desire to survive is very strong. It does not allow the nicety of higher thinking to come in the way of survival. I have become a grown up man now. Here I earn enough to make both ends meet. To satisfy my need of learning, I occasionally go to the missionary school in the evening, but only when I am not too tired. It is a day-to-day living. Instead of the school learning, I am now learning the realities of life and it is a lesson that is very necessary for survival. I do not want to make you sad by my story. There are many like me who live a life of financial uncertainty. Their whole life goes in earning enough to survive. In this competitive world, there is no choice but to be content of what you have rather than spoil your mood for desiring what you cannot have. Please do not think I am a pessimist, because this is the reality.'

A person who wanted to engage him to take his load to the bazaar interrupted his talk. I did not want him to lose this opportunity to make a few rupees. I therefore wished him well and came away sadder. The world had lost a good student to the pangs of hunger.

THE PROSPEROUS ONE

He is a man of wealth. He is important among the very important persons in the country. He is not a millionaire but a multibillionaire. He has a say in the financial affairs of the country. He does not want politics but politics wants him. He supplies the basic material to the industries that produce consumer goods. He is not employed but employs many persons at different levels. He is the source of funds for fighting elections. His reach is far and wide. He flies not with others like him but has his own planes. To know about him you don't call him but read the newspapers. He makes the news with every action of his.

He is one of the wealthiest among the likes of him in the world. He can buy whatever or whoever he likes. He is a successful man. People are afraid of him for the power that he wields.

His shareholders adore him for the difference that he makes in their life. He holds interest in the major industries in the country and the world. When he does not like any policy of the rulers, the babus take note of it and try to adjust. He is not seen often among the common ones. He has a class of his own. He defines wealth and status. He is invited for consultation when policies are to be decided by the business community. He is a leader of the leading lights of business houses. Many industries depend on him. Even the religious institutions look towards him for filling their coffers. Charities are always lining up for his benevolence.

He displays his affluence by the big mansions and un-approachability. The press is afraid of criticizing his ways of working. Even if he manipulates a few individuals here and there, no one has the guts to openly criticize his deeds. He can silence all opposition with the weapon of wealth. The exact amount of his wealth is at best only a guess. Only he knows how much he has. Knowing his wealthy empire no one can say that he comes from a poor country in which forty percent live below the poverty line. He makes the country proud by his inclusion in the list of the world's richest persons. We do not know much about his charitable activities but we believe, since he is a religious person, he must be donating a part of his wealth to that cause.

He is one among the billion where students have to leave their studies for lack of resources and mothers have to put their children to work for buying food. He stands at the one end of spectrum whose other end is total deprivation. God has indeed created a good variety of individuals among the humans.

THEY MAKE OUR LIFE

They make and shape our lives. They are our parents, brothers, sisters, relations, teachers, doctors, friends and colleagues in our working environment. For the middle class life, they are our advisers and they share our secrets. They reflect their personality in what we become. Without their interaction our life is incomplete.

We owe them our gratitude, our respect and our love. They give us an experience of life that we would miss otherwise. We learn from them the skills, and behavior towards others. They teach us the values of life, the sensitivity of society towards certain actions. They provide us fun and amusement. They tell us how to tolerate the unpleasantness in society. They help us to choose our priorities. They make us understand the meaning of affection, concern for others and brotherly bond that unites human beings. They enable us to share our sorrows and disappointments. They laugh and play with us. They provide the anchor in the stormy weather. They lift us from defeat and put us on the path of progress. When we are rudderless, they show us the goal. They instruct, cajole and threaten for our own good. They guide, supervise and sustain us in our difficult times. They make us aware of the pitfalls and show the right path.

They bear our idiosyncrasies, our anger, and our imperfections. They even bear the consequences of our wrong doings. They make us distinguish between true love and mere flattery. They stand by us in our weakness. They lift us from our failures. They provide us the hard ground when we slip on mud.

They do not expect any reward for their help. They are with us because they love us. They do not flinch when we give them pain. They are with us through thick and thin. They do not need nor expect any return gifts. They are ours because we are theirs. They teach us selfless love through example. Even when we ourselves become teachers and doctors, they show us the hereditary structures of ethics and morality. They warn us against temptations.

They give us trust, faith and ideologies. They mould our opinions on matters of interest to us. They do not impose but motivate us to understand the world. They give us the experience of their lives. They are a gift of God to us. God lies within us, but externally He lives in them for our benefit. They are the form of God that we do not worship but befriend. Through them, the God makes us face the world that He has created to experience life. Without them, we would only be crying after birth and no body would listen to us.

Feel their presence and be obliged. You owe them a gratitude you have often neglected to acknowledge. You may not worship God but you owe them respect. They are not things one can buy. You get them by the grace of God. Acknowledge their role and move ahead; all they want is your progress and welfare. Do not deny them the love they seek. Your love to them returns manifold. Love and be loved.

THE DIFFERENT SHADES OF FRIENDSHIP

Friendship is not developed in a day. It grows slowly with understanding. Sometimes it is spontaneous but that is rare. With age, friendship takes different hues. In childhood there is not much reason to be friends. It begins from a necessity to play together. In higher school, it grows out of necessity to be colleagues in study and healthy competition. In college, when the brain is sufficiently developed to understand the needs of the world, friendship takes a different turn. Professional friendship is not all that selfless as in childhood. Friendship of later years is due to commonality of interest. Not many young friends are available in old age.

Childhood friendship is not based on any identity of views. It is primarily based on the desire to seek playmates that are willing to come together. If some one is not a spoilsport he/she is always welcome to join the group. It is for this reason that this friendship does not last long. Another reason may be that new faces come into one's life as one grows, obliterating the memory of those who are no longer as visible as they used to be. I hardly remember any childhood friend at this age except of course that I did have friends that I shared my pre-secondary school days with. They were not of age to advise me anything and shared my company simply because I enjoyed their company. One or two of them shared my background of home atmosphere and were financially in the same condition as I was. I could help some of them in their problems connected with studies while they gave me preference in play. There was no hang-up in anybody of his or her parent's status or social standing. Perhaps such things are out of the minds in children. There is equality in the real sense, which gets diminished with time as brain development proceeds with inputs from parents and society. I remember, one was a street vendor's son while another was the son of a wealthy advocate. We played and laughed together much to our amusement and enjoyment of companionship. No body commented about the clothes, or the pocket money, that one had. All that mattered was unity of interest, coming to the playground and discussing the manner of sharing the time of play. If one fell short of money in buying some edible stuff, the other would contribute without any sense of obliging. If one is to learn about universal brotherhood, one may as well learn it from children.

It is quite painful to see nowadays that the vices of adults are infiltrating with time into the children at an age where they should behave as children and not adults. Perhaps it is the audiovisual media that is responsible for this aberration. The sense of inequality is descending from the parents to the children as fast as the rate of rising prosperity. We no longer find the same innocence that was the characteristic of children some fifty years back. The difference in schooling, the dress and the studying environment is stratifying the children into social groups that we find among the adults. Unknowingly, we are taking away the childlike innocence from our future.

The pressure of the competitive world, the peer pressure, the stresses of society and the absence of ethical and moral values are taking its toll among the future citizens of this world. We no longer care if a child of ten years wants to drive without license, is eager to have a gun, or tries to bully other children by the sheer force of his father's wealth or status. By giving them the toys that are beyond their age, we are turning them into irresponsible and undisciplined bullies. This is in fact a very skewed form of love for the child. If we truly love them we should see them grow in to good citizens who work hard for the welfare of all.

The kind of friendship you have in adolescence is very important from parents' point of view. It can make or break a person's future personality. It is a very critical age for deciding whom to have as a friend. A wrong choice can ruin parent's expectations.

The hormonal changes and growing awareness make this age especially susceptible to asserting oneself and having one's way when there is advice to the contrary. If the friendship supports the wrong path, the person can go downhill never to come again for improvement. But a responsible friendship can mould the ideas of the adolescent to improve one's prospects in future. This is an age of secondary school, and early college. Many a life has been destroyed by falling in bad company in the pursuit of recognition and acceptance in the wrong groups. Wrong habits can form in this age because this is a formative stage of life. One wants to be accepted among the adults as equal and at the same time the mind is not fully mature to understand the implications of wrong habits. Those who have passed through this stage know the importance of caution to be exercised in this critical age. One becomes aware of the physicality of human body and the needs of the body. The temptations are many. But the result of indulgence is rarely anticipated by the growing youth. It is only the parents, teachers or older friends who can provide the necessary guidance that is so relevant at this age.

Friends formed in adolescence tend to go a long way in later life if the visibility of these friends continues. I had about four to five friends that I considered close to me in the secondary school stage. One died as a trainee pilot, another died in college, one became a civil engineer, another a mechanical engineer and one an architect. After three score years, I still cherish this memory since this friendship was based on equality and similarity in thought processes. One of them I met after twenty-five years in separation, but the bond was still as fresh as ever. Another one I am still in correspondence and whenever I meet him, it is a source of pleasure. The friendship of this age is of clear minds and clean hearts. There is no competitive jealousy and no deceitful maneuvers. Every one charts his course of action and others are happy to see his growth in life.

Unlike the friendship of childhood and that of adolescence, the professional friendship is of necessity and self-interest. Sometimes we seek professional friendship to learn the trades or seek one's formula of growth, while at times it is simply to seek company since we loose track of our earlier friends. There is also a spirit of competition that sours friendly relations up to a point. Sometimes in the garb of friendship, the adversary will try to harm to serve his own interest.

Professional relationship is marred by the desire to outwit others in order to gain an upper hand in promotions or to come in the good books of the boss. It is a peculiar linkage. Now very sweet and soft and then going selfish because somebody in the family wants you to step over others. The higher you go the loner you become. If you have to extract work from your erstwhile friends, you cannot be as friendly with them as you would have liked to be. You have to keep appearances of friendship and at the same time to use them to your advantage. That is why some people insist that friendship in profession can only be between equals in status and not otherwise. It can neither be with juniors nor with seniors. Moreover even with equals you have to be sensitive to the sense of competition for further growth.

In my professional life I experienced one of the worst experiences of my life where professional jealousy showed its ugly face. At that time it pained me and I felt hurt. But now in hindsight I find it rather amusing. It just showed how low one could get in the pursuit of one's self interest. One imagines competition where it does not exist. One stoops low to get favors from the seniors. One rides the shoulders of others to look tall. One denigrates others to look better in comparison. Friendship of long duration is thrown away to get bits of crumbs from others. The worst side of human beings becomes visible for small favors and petty promises. Human nature is indeed very fragile. It breaks down at insignificant gains and temporary benefits.

Friendship of old age exists only in name. Actually it is the friendship that lasts over the years. New friendship in old age is scarce. Actually, friends tend to get lost in the old age since one is generally of no use to anybody at that age. Only the very lucky ones can hope to continue having friends in old age. Whoever survives that long has to thank his stars for any kind of friendship that he can get at that age. The desires to talk increases but the listeners dwindle. No body has time to listen to idle talk. People out of self-pride in their intelligence; do not want to listen to advice. The old people too think that they can advise others about their own experiences and others should listen to them. It is a strange sight when older people want to talk but the listeners tend to ignore on one pretext or the other. Nature plays strange tricks. Longevity of a person has no relationship with the utility of the person. Great thinkers and reformers died young while insignificant persons live long. I do not want to look disrespectful to old age for it has a storehouse of wisdom, but the tragedy is that no body is interested in that wisdom. Everybody, in his ego, thinks himself or herself great.

Life is a paper boat sailing on the river of nature
Carrying dreams, half filled and half empty

When the boat rocked, I asked, 'what happens to my dreams?'
A voice replied, ' dreaming is a continuous process,
Do not worry about the loss. Start dreaming again
For time never stops.'

I listened to the voice
And started living again.

OPINIONS

RIGHT AND WRONG

Very often one is torn between conflicting decisions and is unable to say what is right and what is wrong. This indecision is a direct result of clashing of interests. If we are objective, free of emotions and unmindful of our self-interest, it is much easier to take the right decision. But most often we are unable to decide because we are not fair to our conscience, which is the true indicator of right decision. We superimpose our self-interest on our voice of conscience and find innumerable excuses to curb it. We try to justify wrong decision on one argument or the other. Our intelligence helps in this process of denying the conscience its true place. We argue about the practicality of our decision in the context of imperfect world. We tell ourselves that if we listen to the conscience, our family may suffer. We look for examples where in similar circumstances how other people behaved, not realizing that they too must have succumbed to pressures such as self gain, family's interest and so on. We hardly exercise our discerning faculty that is based on dispassionate thinking and intuitive thought.

Why do we not develop our conscience to guide us out of most of our difficult situations? Why are we afraid to follow its guidance? The reason is simple. Its advice is generally in line with universal application and not for catering to your interest alone. Those who are habituated to seek their selfish ends cannot agree with its advice. Conscience becomes strong if we usually listen to it and act accordingly. But if we ignore it more often, then it tends to become silent. A silent conscience is an easy gateway to wrong decision or at best selfish decisions.

To make the conscience strong, we must act according to universal values of life. It is the voice of God that resides within you. God will never deceive you and will always guide you correctly in the interest of universal good. It is the personal interest that overrides it and masks its voice of reason. The spiritually oriented person has a highly developed conscience that goes in the name of *Vivek*, the ability to discern correctly. It removes all doubts that basically arise due to conflicting interests.

If people led pure lives, there is no reason to go astray. Their intuitive faculties will improve and their judgment of events and people will generally be right. The discerning ability and the intuitive faculty overlap in our personality. This region is the start of divine thought. The divine thought is never considered wrong for the simple reason that it relates to the divine will to do well to all. It is part of universal will. The more we universalize our thought, the closer we go to the mind of God. Universal consciousness is part of divine consciousness. This is the starting ladder for spiritual experience that leads to God consciousness. The path of spiritual thinking is not only for the saints; it is very much relevant to our daily life of contradictions, indecisive situations and our need to be clear headed. If you develop your conscience with spiritual way of life, it is going to pay dividends in your mundane matters as well. Always remember that conscience is the voice of God.

LOVE AND HATRED

Universal love is a soothing emotion while hatred is a negative emotion that agitates the mind. Universal love at once puts you on equality with others while hatred is individualized and directed against specific persons. Universal love is divine in nature; hatred is demonic when it leads to violence. If you love others, you are loved by all. Hatred too is reactive, it is returned in the same manner. But if you return love against hatred, you nullify the negativity and spread peace all around. Just as love and compassion are related emotions, hatred and anger too have a relation.

Universal love and love for an individual are different. Love for an individual has an expectation. It generally demands love in return. But universal love has no such expectation. It is spiritually oriented. There is equality in its spread. It arises from the feeling that same reality is present in all and hence there is no difference between the lover and the beloved. This universal love is equated to love for God. In fact some call this universal love itself as the manifestation of God. Saints and mystics have always emphasized the cultivation of this universal love as the aim of God realization. In bhakti too, the love for individual form of God has to be sublimated to universal love. The universal love has infinite dimension while the individualized love is restricted to one. Love of God is infinite. Human love is restricted to preferences and desires. In order to reach the level of God-consciousness, human love must expand to universal love.

Universal love has no scope for any hatred or anger. If your love for humanity is universalized, there is no scope left for hatred or anger because universal love embraces all. In universal love you tend to ignore the faults of others because then no one is considered as the other. All are then included in 'I'. The same spirit reigns supreme, full of love, compassion and equality. There is only oneness and no otherness.

Hatred arises from restricting our emotions to specific persons. There is no universal hatred as such. As soon as we indulge in hatred we restrict our sphere from the limitless to a limited form of existence. From infinite we come down to finite. This applies to all negative emotions. Negativity is a symbol of our restricted life. We come down from universal existence to narrow minded life of individualized egoistic creatures. We start thinking of you and me. Hatred is a form of selfish living. We start believing in self-interest as the prime need of our existence. Our thoughts become more human than divine. Individual ego is differentiating. Universal thought is integrating. The process of becoming divine from human is to change our thought processes from individual to universal.

When we love every one as a form of God, we universalize our thoughts. When we hate a person as an undesirable being, we are reducing ourselves to finite humans riddled with ego and selfish thought. We no longer then act in the image of God. God is universal, humans is finite. Negativity imposes limits on our life and thoughts. A universal mind is in sync with the mind of God. The spiritual process extends our horizon of thought from the limited to the limitless. It is a process that turns us humans to divine existence. Changing hatred to love helps in this transformation.

SUCCESS AND FAILURE

Success and failure are related to an aim. If the aim is achieved, you are successful otherwise you fail. Aims differ with different people. Some aim to achieve a high position, others wealth or social recognition. In different walks of life, the aims differ. Therefore, the measure of success is not unique. For one person, earning a million may be the aim, for another it may be a billion. Both may be successful in their own way. Some people keep their aim very high and try to achieve as much as they can. Their measure of success depends on their level of contentment and not on the totality of the desired aim of achievement..

I remember two cases in which the objective of both was to rise in career but different methods were employed to achieve it. In one case, the person was happy go lucky with not much intelligence or high academic record but possessing a keen desire to achieve his objective by any means, fair or foul. In the other case, the person was academically strong but with attachment to principles of ethics and morality. Both of them achieved a position more or less the same but with different tactics. One employed flattery and sycophancy while the other used his knowledge without flattering any one. Though both seemed to be successful in their own way there was a marked difference in their ways of working. If we go by the results achieved, there is not much to choose between them as far as success is concerned. But if we choose the means adopted, there was a world of difference.

If we concern ourselves with success both in terms of means and ends, then definition of success should run as 'achieving the goal with fair means'. But in the world of today where end is more important than the means, the definition of success seems to be skewed in favor of result achieved, no matter with what means. This shows the difference between the spiritual working and the working with no holds barred. In spiritual terms, success means 'achievement with right methods'. But in practical situations we find success to mean 'with whatever means that are available'. This is the reason for the values of life giving ground to unethical methods. We have changed our thought patterns to suit convenience. It is much harder to achieve success by keeping our values of life intact. There are umpteen temptations to shed ethics and go for easy routes. Most people opt for this. But there are some who still think that life is not all about success in mundane sense but it is about keeping spiritual values intact. If you believe in reincarnation, the life span of our existence in this body is a small part of our supposedly eternal existence. What we achieve here does matter but only a little in the overall context of multi-life existence.

There was a time when majority believed in the values of life. But our obsession with success has downgraded the importance of ethics and morality in the pursuit of success. Failure is considered a sin. To achieve success by hook or by crook is accepted in society as the done thing. Spiritual values are seen to be talked about but not practiced. Every body is in a mad rush to achieve success by any means. Acquisition of wealth and status has become synonymous with success. In the pursuit of goal, means are ignored. We have yet to learn the meaning of right living.

FLOWERS AND THORNS

Everybody loves flowers for their smell, their beauty and the softness of their petals. No body loves thorns for they prick and cause pain. But both flowers and thorns are nature's gift to man. Nature wants us to live with both; they are a fact of life. Many plants have both flowers and thorns existing side by side.

Flowers adorn the places of worship, social functions, celebrations, birthday parties and funerals. They are offered out of respect, with love and with reverence. They are a symbol of friendship, concern, and faith. When offered to the sick, they give a moment of happiness and provide a diversion to the depressed. When put in the flowerpot in a house they spread fragrance all around. They add to the beauty of the maiden. They represent the feelings of the lover to the beloved, be it the human or the divine. Flowers are a source of inspiration to the poet.

Thorns are an object of fear and hate. The sharp pointed thorns are avoided for their prickly pain that accompanies the oozing of blood. The touch of a thorn causes a curse to the unknown for the stinging feeling. Nobody plants roses, bougainvilleas and cacti for the thorns but they are an essential accompaniment of the flowers. You cannot have the goodness of roses without the unpleasantness of thorns. But thorny bushes do have a place in boundaries for stopping the intruders.

Nothing in nature is useless. Every thing has a use. All creation is an outcome of a universal intelligence that evolves and perfects every thing. Human brain is the best creation. Nature has provided a great asset to the human being. But its use requires a caution. It can do great harm if used indiscriminately. It applies equally to all objects that provide power to man.

When a thorn pricked me, I cursed the plant
The plant whispered to me and said in a lamenting tone,
'I am sorry for the pain,
But how else can I protect my flowers
And safeguard them from the cruel humans
They come and pluck the buds and flowers
And leave me crying with the separation,
I lose my friendship with the birds and bees
Who come for the flowers and give me company
In the absence of flowers, I am left with the thorns to cry.
The humans don't realize the flowers have a long life with me
Without me, they wither away in a day
While in my lap they live for days, smiling and laughing with the wind.
The humans have lost touch with nature
And want every thing to serve them
They have no sense of equality with other creation.
So with small pricks, I remind them
To live with me, in peace, and enjoy the creation.'

CRUELTY AND COMPASSION

Cruelty takes many forms. Physical violence, speech violence and thought violence. Most people in anger do physical violence. It is also resorted by the invaders and dacoits in search of wealth. They loot and plunder what comes in their way. Most of medieval conquerors were nothing short of looters who subjugated the innocent citizens in the name of conquering the territory. They ruled with cruelty and levied taxes.

Speech violence hurts for a long time since it touches the sensitivity of a person. Speech violence originates from an inborn hatred towards others and sometimes has a deeper effect than physical violence. It pierces the heart like an arrow. The wise have always warned against using abusive language for it rankles in the mind of the person for a long time.

Thought violence concerns entertaining and planning deceit, misguidance and similar modes of harm. Cunning thoughts in the name of cleverness come under this negative approach to human interaction. Even sweet talk with the aim of taking advantage of the person can be classed under this heading. Sympathetic speech and action with a black heart characterize this attitude.

History is a witness to the fact that cruelty has been perpetrated in the name of religion, national interest and plain maintenance of law and order. Cruelty also arises from a fear complex where self-survival is threatened. Cruelty under a dictatorship is well known. Cruelty however is not confined to rulers alone. Cruelty under domestic environment and crowd entertainment is also seen. Wherever power is unchallenged, it is likely to deteriorate to cruel administration.

Compassion is an ennobling experience. It is a sign of one's confidence in oneself and confidence in the goodness of human heart. It shows a fearless attitude to life. One wants to share the good things of life with others. It combines love and empathy for others. Compassionate attitude signals the rise of spirituality in the person. It is one of the universal values of life. All religions emphasize this virtue to be cultivated by all the followers of the religion. It, however, requires courage to be loving and compassionate in the face of cruelty and injustice. Only the very brave can adhere to this virtue when confronted by unjust actions or abusive attitude. Forgiveness is an associated virtue and you cannot be compassionate if you do not have the will and strength to forgive. Anger management is also necessary to be compassionate and forgiving. The virtues of love, compassion, and forgiveness arise from the development of strength of character. Only the brave and selfless can be successful in developing these values.

A weak-minded person is always afraid of speaking his mind in truth and honesty that is so essential for being mentally brave. A clear conscience gives the person the required strength to be brave in expression and right action. Fearlessness is a quality of honest persons. The guilty and the deceitful are always evasive in their dealings with people. They can hardly afford the luxury of transparency in their behavior. They move in dark channels to take advantage of others, without ever sharing the credit with them.

PRIDE AND HUMILITY

Pride is a manifestation of ego. Whether individualized or collective, it displays a sense of achievement in the worldly way. In the case of a nation or a country, the collective pride appears in the form of nationalism. Self-pride is good for moving ahead in life. National pride is necessary for the advancement of a country.

In spiritual sphere, it is humility that is given more importance than pride. Pride isolates a person as an individual. Humility shows the understanding of an individual in relation to the vast creation, the macro cosmos, in relation to the human being. Humility should not be seen in the light of lowliness. A great person can also be a humble person. All great saints have been very humble persons.

In the active world, ego based pride gives self-confidence and a drive to achieve more. It fulfills the desire to move ahead of others. Great achievements are made by persons of pride in order to stay ahead and win the praise of others. Humility can also win the praise if a great achievement is seen in perspective. Pride of achievement and the shallow self-importance, are two different things.

Spiritually speaking, when you see the same God residing in everybody, you find equality with every one. In that frame of mind, pride dissolves and gives way to humility since you find, including yourself, a life in the image of the same reality that pervades every where. Such a person can never boast of his superiority or even have a pride of his achievement since he offers every action to that reality. He thinks that every action of his is in response to the will of that reality. He lives by the will of God and not by his egoistic desires of individual existence. He joins his will with the will of Supreme.

Humility helps a lot in shedding ego. It is an essential trait of great spiritual souls. Humility is not a sign of weakness, as most people believe. It is an acceptance of limited and finite existence of an individual. Those who practice humility realize their limitation in comparison to the limitless and eternal reality that is behind all creation. They know that their boast will be laughable in the light of uncertain future that lies ahead. Boastful people have often come to grief.

Pride in the sense of boast is not desirable. Pride in the achievement is acceptable for personal advancement as it boosts the confidence. But humility with achievement is the true indicator of a mature person. Nature also tells us to be humble when you have something to give to others. A tree laden with fruit has always its branches drooping towards the ground.

The difference between pride and humility is best illustrated by the difference in the temperament of the kings and the saints. The pride drives the kings to conquer others though physical power. The saints conquer others through spiritual power. What matters, and lasts longer, is the winning of heart and not the winning of physical body.

INTELLIGENT AND CLEVER

I believe the world is given direction by the intelligent and run by the clever. Intelligent people who are academically brilliant and have the capacity to understand quickly the intricacies of any subject make the discoveries in science and arts. The clever people make good money and know how to go about the affairs of the world. They can understand the minds of people well and can maneuver the ways of the world nicely. These are however the two well to do sections of society who influence the life of ordinary people in a big way. People who are intelligent and clever belong to a rare breed.

Intelligent people are rather shy of social interactions. They confine themselves to the subject of interest and rarely understand the machinations of the clever people. Unless they have the family resources, they can hardly manage the financial side of their life. The clever people, on the other hand, rarely worry about the academic problems. They are practical people who know how to move about in the mud and slush of life. They understand the pulse of the common man and act accordingly to serve their interest. They are the politicians and the businessmen, who by virtue of the power they hold run the affairs of the state.

Intelligent people philosophize and discover the truths behind life and the creation. They are the one to discover the reality behind this material world. They set the values of life. The comment on and propagate the concepts that matter. Their theories provide the input for people to direct their lives. They are also the ones who enter controversies with other intelligent people because of the strong views they hold. The clever people shun controversies. They rarely come into limelight and remain behind the curtain to exercise the power they wield. Their thinking never becomes clear to the ordinary man. They manage to grab contracts and make money in myriad ways. They are fond of socializing and throw big parties because they thrive on other people. They patronize arts and are the bread giver to the ordinary man.

The intelligent start intellectual movements and clever ones use these movements to their purpose. The intelligent ones are the creators of technology and clever ones use that technology to make money. The clever are the employers of technical people. They provide the money for the exploitation of the output of intelligent people.

Society needs the services of both the intelligent and the clever. Every country needs technological advancement and wealth generation. These two sections of society are the trendsetters and the rest of the community follows them. The world of today runs on brainpower. Both the intelligent and the clever use their brain albeit in different directions. They are the essential components of modern society. If any one of these two sections is suppressed in preference to the other, the result is bound to be retrograde. The clever should not overpower the intelligent because they are the creators off new thought. Life runs on change. Unless new thoughts are generated, the progress cannot proceed. The clever generate the wealth. One is the backbone and the other is the flesh. The body needs both.

THE IDEAL AND THE PRACTICAL

It is important to have some ideal in life to make it worthwhile. It is however very difficult to live by it. The practical person lives by his needs and has no set ideas to stick to. For him what matters is to have his way in the journey of life, no matter how many deviations he has to undertake. To have an ideal provides a direction to the life. Sooner or later, the idealist earns respect for following a principled life. The practical may run a smooth life but lack of ideal makes his life a bit meaning less.

The idealist frequently faces obstacles in life because the views he holds may not agree with others. His sticking to the ideal may even annoy some people. But such a person does have something to live for. The practical one moulds his views according to the circumstances in order to suit his interests. There is no fixed set of rules for him to run his life. He may change his colors according to the direction in which the wind blows. There is a crisis of faith in the case of the practical one since he has no set of rules by which he is known to respond. On the other hand, one is quite sure about the mind of the idealist since his views are generally well known.

At times the idealist finds himself quite aloof in holding onto his ideal. The opposition to his view may make him a loner. But such persons are of strong character and can withstand criticism. The practical one is a smooth operator. When faced with difficulties, he slides into solutions quite smoothly.

The idealist thinking leads to reforms; that is why most reformers are great idealists. This includes religious leaders and social reformers. Even though some of their ideas may not be very practicable, they stick to them with great zeal. For example, committed reformers have tried uprooting bribery and corruption and adulteration in foodstuff but these vices remain in society in spite of their best efforts. This is because society can never be rid of bad elements completely. Similarly there are other social evils that so many idealist thinkers try to remove, but their efforts at best reduce the evils to some extent but not completely.

Idealism stands on a high pedestal that is unconnected with the reality of life. Practical people understand this and try to remain away from controversial thinking. They somehow bypass controversy and go about doing their work with unconcern und noninvolvement. Their aim in life is to get what they want without raising any hassles or arguments.

If you wish to find the idealist and the practical in profession, you may try the philosophers and businessmen. The philosophers will go on exhorting people to stand by certain principles but businesspersons keep going in their work without bothering much about these lofty ideals. The latter will even grease the palms of officials for the completion of their aims if such eventualities have to be faced. If the idealists were not there, the society will lose its soul to sheer commercialism. That is why nature provides all shades of opinion in society to keep a balance.

THE GREEDY AND THE GENEROUS

Greed is an urge to gather more than what is genuinely needed. It is a negative desire that needs to be curbed. In fact, greed has no limits. A greedy person does not know when to stop desiring more. In nature, if you take more than what you need, you are trampling on somebody else's rights of possession. When it happens, you cause waste as well as deprivation. Greed is a negative quality that needs to be suppressed in the interest of spreading the resources evenly among the needy.

A generous person willfully gives to others what he does not need. It is a positive trait and is appreciated by one and all. A generous person benefits others and earns the blessings of the needy. You can be generous without harming your own interests. In the religious codes of most religions, it is prescribed that one should give in charity about ten to fifteen percent of his wealth to the needy. By doing this he earns the blessings of God and is respected in society for his generosity.

In a given sample of people you can always find the greedy and the generous coexisting, for nature likes to have variety in creation. The generous compensate to some extent the problems created by the greedy. One thing about greed is that it multiplies ad infinitum once it gets into the head, there is no check on it and it grows and grows. Ultimately it rebounds on the person and causes his downfall. A greedy person is a pitiable sight. Even if he is surrounded by deprivation, he seldom checks himself since he becomes a prisoner of his desires. His greed makes him insensitive to the needs of others. He merely becomes an instrument for excessive acquisition and hoarding. No amount of wealth satisfies him. There is only one point agenda in his life and that is to get more and more. Contentment is unknown to him. Even if some spiritually oriented person reminds him of the need to be contented, he ignores the advice and goes on his mission of acquiring more and more.

The saints have repeatedly told us that we should treat the worldly wealth as a gift of God, to be kept temporarily with us as custodians and not as owners. Ultimately every thing belongs to nature. The idea of owning land or money permanently is wrong. Land does not belong permanently to anyone. It is at best a matter of a few generations. The conquerors of land that felt proud of owning a country or a state are no longer alive to claim their rights. The feet of time trample every bit of their possessions into dust. Even their descendents fade away with time. A generation lasts hardly fifty years and the new generation does not have the same love for the acquisitions of their forefathers because they get it without spending any effort. In the hearts of people, generosity lasts much longer compared to the greed.

Generosity is one of the desirable qualities of a spiritual person. It arises from the feeling of equality among all persons. If you love a person, you want to share everything of yours with that person. If you love all, you would like to take only that which is necessary for you and leave the rest for others. Generosity, giving and sharing are positive traits of a civilized person. Looting, snatching and hoarding are the traits of an uncivilized person. If we claim ourselves to be part of a civilized society, let us learn to be generous in giving and shun the greed.

OUR LONELINESS

One night in my dream, I asked God why are we so lonely in universe?
We are searching for so many years but have not found
Another planet with life like our own. Are you not happy with our performance?

He replied, ' I wanted to create heaven on earth,
With nature's beauty, lakes, rivers, hills and valleys
With forests, flowers, fruits and green foliage
With marine life, colored fish and coral reefs
All this for humans to enjoy
In peace, togetherness and joyous existence

But look what humans have done
They have used the resources with selfish greed,
Killed others for selfish gain
Depleted forests and seas,
Polluted water and air
Cut forests for ugly buildings

Used intelligence to make
Deadly weapons and waged wars
Created boundaries between man and man
Replaced love with hatred and envy
Divided men on castes and religions
Generated philosophies to disown me
Argued about my intentions
Played one against another in ignorance
Created dissentions between men and women
Exploited children and fought on flimsy grounds

They have literally created hell on my intended heaven.
They now intend to mine other planets for resources
They speak untruth in the name of truth
They have created a class of politicians
Who exploit men in the name of nationalism
They have legalized greed and self-interest
They impose their thoughts on others
They have multiplied religions in the name of humanism
They cause barriers in trade and commerce,
In language and customs, in color and religion
They politicize in my name and feel proud in conversion

You tell me why should I multiply their weaknesses elsewhere
If given a long rope they will fight interplanetary wars
And destroy the universe with nuclear weapons
I feel it is unwise to duplicate those who create hell out of heaven.

PROFESSIONAL DIGNITY

BODY HEALERS

'What do you do for a living?' I asked.

'I heal people and bring them out of pain and suffering;' he replied.

'That is surely a very noble activity. You must be a very satisfied person, because not many people get this opportunity of serving people in such a way.' I continued.

'I don't think you are completely right. These days people seem to have lost the respect that was there a few years ago for this profession.' He was rather unhappy to continue, but elaborated, 'you see, somehow the families of patients believe that they are paying hefty sums and therefore it is their right to demand continuous service without any obligation. Any slip on the part of persons involved is seen as a deliberate negligence. If the person does not respond to treatment it is seen as the fault of the healer. Every other day you find incidents between the medical staff and the patients' families that boil over to headlines in newspapers. The incidents are becoming ugly and violent. It is a sorry state of affairs that affects the morale of workers and the affected families. The situation is so bad that there are frequent strikes and posting of law enforcement agencies to prevent untoward incidents. Obviously there is too much expectation from healers who are after all humans and as such have limitations of their own. The commitment of the support staff may not match with that of the doctors, but they have to bear the brunt of the overall deficiency in attendance. The working conditions also may be difficult because too many patients are chasing too few doctors. The poor sanitation, too many family members accompanying the patient and crowding the hospitals are some of the reasons for tempers going high.'

'But you will agree that there are some black sheep in the profession who display a greed for money and exploit the innocent people for their own advantage. There may also be some negligence on the part of professionals and incompetence on the part of attending doctors genuinely which triggers people,' I provoked him intentionally to have his view.

'Yes, that is likely but then it applies to most professions', he said. 'You cannot blame the profession for that. The medical profession deals with the most complex creation of nature, the living being. It is not like repairing a machine. In addition to the body there are psychological factors to care for. The concern of the doctor is not less than that of the patient's family. He is bound by his professional ethics to treat and monitor the progress of the patient. But he is not God. He too has his limitation. He too has his family to care for. He too has to have some rest to be fit again. People think once they come to hospital, nothing should go wrong. They forget that nature too plays its part. After the surgery, it is only the nature that heals the wounds. The doctor does his best and the nature does the rest.'

I realized that what he said had an element of truth. I therefore said, 'may be the problem lies in the lack of information to the concerned parties that have high emotional stake. It is for the administration to keep the progress of the patient known at every step to the concerned family members. To avoid any ugly situation, both the healer and the patient have to cooperate.'

THE HEALER OF SOUL

'I feel soul healing is as important as the healing of body because the present thinking is that body and mind form one unit and soul is intimately related to one's thinking process.' I said this when confronted by a holy person who had returned from a lecture course on spirituality.

He said he agreed with me but there were certain difficulties in healing soul as related to body healing. He said, 'one of the most striking point is that while body healing solely depends on the doctor's initiative and his prescription to the patient, soul healing cannot be achieved without an equal effort on the part of the person to be healed. Without the cooperation and sincere effort on the part of the 'soul patient', the soul healer can achieve nothing.'

'Yes I agree to that, but in the present circumstances, the soul healers are getting into difficulty because every other day we find one scandal or another catching the headlines that give a bad name to the places of spiritual healing. People seem to be losing confidence in the credentials of soul healers that are multiplying like mushrooms. All sorts of people seem to ride this bandwagon in the hope of getting riches and fame by associating with spiritual teachers of one hue or another. There is no standard to go by and any body that is vocal and read a few scriptures is preaching spirituality to the innocent common man. There is no yardstick by which we can measure the spiritual depth of the preacher.

The result is that sooner or later one succumbs to his human weakness and brings a bad name to the profession.'

'You are right in what you say. But spirituality is one subject in which practical experience is as important as the theory. Unless a person has followed the path, and reached the goal oneself, one is totally unfit to teach the others. There is no college degree to show the spiritual capability of the teacher. It is a personal experience that the student must have in order to gain from the teaching.'

'I do not deny this. My point is about the bad publicity that spoils the dignity of the profession. Granting that with increased exposure to such tangy and saucy news, the bad publicity spreads like wild fire, the fact remains that unscrupulous persons get entry to this profession and there is no agency to stop the entry of such persons. At times it appears that this is one area that con masters effectively utilize. When their greed and lust get exposed, they move to another place to start again.'

'I have always rated this profession as a noble profession at par with teaching and medicine. But when such incidents appear in news, the faith is shattered and one does not know where to go in search of right persons. People normally turn to such persons and places when they are under the weather psychologically. They need reassurance about the utility of life and a promise for good afterlife. But when they get cheated, their situation becomes worse than before. Loss of faith is more damaging than loss of money. Somehow these days the noble professions seem to be losing their sheen. The trend needs to be reversed in the interest of general public.'

THE TEACHER

'Teaching is another noble profession that is getting devalued in the present age where every thing is weighed in terms of money. Increasingly people are feeling that they pay and get education without any obligation. The teacher, they think is just another employee and deserves no better consideration.'

I said this to my colleague who took offence at this remark and said, 'is not the teacher becoming unduly aware of his rights and payments like any wage earner? I feel, gone are the days when a teacher exemplified dedication and commitment to his student. These days they have unions like any labor force. They fight for better pay packages and use their spare time for taking extra classes on payment. The extra coaching has become a big business that challenges the very school system. Students are more worried about getting a seat in competitive exams rather than learning the subject in the regular school system. The teachers feel they can make more money in the coaching environment than in making commitment to the students.'

' You may be right in criticizing the system but remember that teaching used to be the most respected profession in earlier days. People had full faith in the powers of the teacher to not only teach the academics but also put the student on ethical way of life. This latter element of civilizing the student has almost vanished from the curriculum of teaching these days. The result is that we have more bullies coming out of school than good citizens of society. The teacher has lost the respect and reverence that he once commanded. The absenteeism, the lack of moral education and loss of discipline have eroded the teacher-student bond that used to be so strong. Respect is something that cannot be demanded but has to be earned.'

'You are indeed right in connecting the downfall of student teacher relationship to lack of discipline in schools, but remember that in this age of buying and selling education, people think that they can buy degrees as they buy the ration or the cloth. This changed thinking is detrimental to the standard of education. Today universities are coming up like grocery shops. From one-room universities you can hardly expect world standards. The number of degree holders is rising but the competence level is falling. No wonder then the degree is getting devalued. The employers as well as the degree holders are getting disillusioned with the system.'

'I don't think those who contemplate the improvement in education system have any concern for raising the respect level of teachers. Merely raising the pay structure or perks cannot restore the respect in the hearts of students. It is only the teachers that can reverse the downfall by improving the commitment and hard work that will bring back the respect to the profession that it deserves. When that dignity and respect returns in the minds of people, the evils in the system will automatically evaporate. The teachers, students and common people have all to give their best to improve the situation; otherwise the nobility of profession will vanish forever. It will be a sad day if and when it happens.'

THE LAW

Maintenance of law and order is an important element of civilized existence. Along with justice, it imparts a dignity to citizens. It is invariably linked to respect and fear of the law enforcing agencies; respect for the givers of justice and fear of the maintainers of law that bring law breakers to justice. This is the single most important factor for peace in society. Without this important element, no section of society can feel safe and be able to carry on its work.

Any distortion in the working of law maintenance reflects badly on the governing agency. Faith in the law-maintaining agency is a must. This faith is critically dependent on the integrity of the officials that are responsible for maintenance of law. Justice and equality are foundations of good governance. The kings in the olden days took great care to this aspect. Many kings are known to go great lengths in giving the people a just and equal law, which was ruthlessly implemented with a fair and just system. Any laxity in this is a source of trouble.

Any defect in the law-maintaining agency causes ripples that stretch far and wide. Any loss of faith is a source of trouble, which makes people restless. If the law enforcers themselves break the law, the freedom of people is jeopardized. The integrity of every one connected with the system is of utmost importance. But we know that this is quite impossible because in every section of society there are always some black sheep that spoil the pack. This has been the problem through the centuries of human existence. Human nature being what it is, to get all the concerned persons of impeccable integrity is very difficult. That is where the dignity of the profession takes a rap. Even if point one percent of the system is bad, the whole system gets the blame. That is why it is often stated that no innocent one should ever be punished even if some bad ones are let free.

The work of the law-maintaining agencies is quite tough. They have to deal with rough and tough bad elements that have scant respect for human life. The lawbreakers do not understand the language of civilized life. They have to be dealt firmly and justly. This puts the officials to risk of life and possibility of getting a bad name in the bargain. They are particularly at a disadvantage if the lawbreakers have high connections. To maintain dignity of profession under such circumstances is indeed very difficult. This is why they stand at a disadvantage compared to other professions.

Those who enter the law maintaining agencies, it is important that they have respect for universal value system of truth, compassion and justice. They cannot afford to be unduly emotional nor jealous. Their psychological back up has to be strong. They must believe in the brotherhood of mankind. They must not have any wrong ideas about their superiority or any unjust pride of their power. Law enforcement is a responsible job that needs to be given to the right persons. A mistake here can prove quite costly to the society.

Respect for law and respect for humanity are similar feelings that need to be nurtured among the masses. No society can afford to ignore it.

THE RESEARCHER

Research in humanities or science has always attracted the most talented and intelligent students. The student comes to research out of interest and not for simply finding a lucrative avenue for wealth. The field of research demands absolute sincerity and total commitment to the field of investigation. That is why only a few come to this field of activity. The results of investigation lead the humanity towards growth and knowledge. It is an area of activity that requires high level of intelligence and a desire to contribute to the society for future advancement. For this reason, the research activity has a dignity of its own.

Scientific researcher is the backbone of research in basic sciences, which in turn leads to development of technology. Technology in turn leads to wealth generation, which drives the economy. This pattern of economic development is so visible in the western developed world. The third world is only imitating this pattern for their growth. This pattern however requires high degree of integrity in research.

Plagiarism in research is a phenomenon that degrades the quality of research and leads to a crisis of confidence in the integrity of the researcher. It also brings a bad name to the institution where research is conducted. Many a researcher has faced this blot in their career and brought disgrace to them and their institution. What is important is not the quantity of research output but the quality of research.

The social relevance of the research output is also important since it directly affects the humanity at large. The possibility of misuse however cannot be foreseen in many cases. It is the intention of users that determines the damage to the society. Most research output that has military application in mind is against the social relevance. It harms the prestige of scientific research and makes people wary of research scientists. Weapons research is driving the economy of some states that threaten to destroy mankind.. This definitely lowers the dignity of research as a profession..

What really has added to the prestige and glory of scientific research is the advancement in medical sciences and the astronomical research that has widened our knowledge about our place in the universe. It has broken so many myths and beliefs. We now are more realistic about our place on earth. It has made us more humble and more aware of our responsibility for sustaining and saving this living planet in the universe. We are now eager to find company in this vast cosmos that stretches beyond the imagination of an ordinary person. Thanks to this research, we know now what infinity means.

Research needs an open mind and a willingness to accept divergent opinion. A closed mind can never find anything new. In this sense, religion and science do not find a common ground. Taking religious statements as the final truth does not help the cause of religion. Investigation must always be encouraged and promoted. Intuitive thinking should not put a stop to investigation of truth.. The dignity of religious truth will indeed enhance if it is supported by evidence gathered through alternative routes. Let religion absorb the lessons learnt through scientific research.

THE MIGRATION

'As far as I know, you were trained as an engineer and your brother as a doctor from highly reputed institutions. But now I find both of you in professions that require only common sense and no technical inputs. Don't you think both of you have betrayed your earlier training for power and wealth. In doing so you have wasted precious resources of the country, which trained you for technical jobs.

Personally speaking, I am quite disappointed to see this migration from technical to non-technical jobs.'

'There is no need to be so disappointed since every one goes for money and power these days. These jobs are also not easy to get. The stress level is also not less. The present jobs carry an equal responsibility if not more. As far as training is concerned we have also been trained for the present jobs. What does it matter to the country if we serve in the present jobs and not in the previously trained ones? We are giving our best to the present jobs and hope to generate wealth for the country. The engineer and the doctor serve no better than the manager or the administrator. All are important for the prosperity of the country.'

'You are missing the point. This country spent quite a sum for your and your brother's training as engineer and doctor. But now all that training has gone waste as far as service to the country is concerned. You moved to a managerial position in a private job while your brother joined government administration. Is it not a waste of resources and money?

'It is a free country and every body is free to pursue any line of activity. I have as much right to choose a career I like as any other person. As far as country is concerned I remain in this land to serve. There are many who use this country's resources for training and then go out to serve other lands. At least my brother and I are doing better than that.. Don't tell me money is not important. Money gives me power and respect. Why should I not opt for that? My idea of national interest is different from yours. The days of conservative thought are over. Happiness results from satisfaction, and we are satisfied.'

'O.K. I agree. It is the satisfaction that matters. If you are satisfied with your action, I am no body to question your intentions. But I suggest you view the situation from the point of those who support engineering and medical training with their taxes. Also consider the plight of those who clamor for admission to engineering and medical seats but can't get admission. I can only wish you and others like you to ponder over the matter and realize the problem at the national level.'

THE ARTIST

An artist is a person of feelings. He /she expresses the feelings through the medium of painting, sculpture, theatre or music. The dignity of the artist lies in standing alone as a person of talent, deep emotions and in the impression that his art makes on people. Of all the professions this is the most expressive and individualistic. Not all people can succeed in this profession without having the desired talent. It is a profession of the select few. The success depends on how articulate the person is through the medium of his expression.

The artist survives on the connection he makes with the feelings of others. He lives in the world of emotions. He is sensitive and sentimental. He easily gets hurt if his art does not touch the hearts of people. An appreciative audience thrills him. His emotional content can raise him to spiritual heights more easily than those who rely on intelligence or cleverness.

For an artist, theatre and cinema is a medium of artistic expression and not of entertainment alone. For him the distinction between classical and modern art is of no relevance. What matters is the art and its expression. In matters of art he is truly universal. Folk art impresses him as much as the classical arts. He is a free bird; he is less concerned with conventions of society and more with freedom and liberty.

An artisan is also an artist when he creates an object of art. The artist in him shines through his work. An object of admiration created by an artist or artisan gives emotional pleasure to every one. A thing of beauty gives dignity to the work and the workman. The artisan is justifiably proud of his work when it pleases the eyes of the beholder and meets the utility for which it is made For all artists and artisans the praise of their work is itself the reward. They derive satisfaction from it. The ego in them is satisfied by the praise and drives them to do better. Every artisan, in fact, has a streak of artist in him. It only needs to flower by encouragement and patronage. In olden times, the kings and wealthy merchants provided the patronage to the artists. Now, in the absence of kings, the rich and the government have taken this role.

The value of art increases with the wealth of the people. A poor country can hardly sustain the arts, as there are other areas of concern that need looking after. Appreciation of art has been traditionally confined to the upper strata of society. They use art as a means of storing their wealth. In that sense, gold, jewels and works of art are important elements of investment.

Art signifies the culture of a country. Absence of artists and artisans reflects poorly on the status of a country. We judge the culture from the standard of art and the artists that give a meaning to life. Any country that does not respect its artists and their work does not deserve to be included in the civilized category of people.

THE BUILDER

On way to my place of work, a huge multistoried structure has come up. It houses many pigeonhole looking flats serving as residences of people. Not all flats seem to be occupied for the reason that the price of each flat is above the reach of ordinary people. The builder is not unduly worried because his margin of profit is such that even partial occupation is enough to give him good gain.

I often wonder whom should I call the builder of this monstrous structure; the person who invested the money, the architect who designed it or the huge labor force that contributed their might to raise it to its present state. It is a structure of the wealthy, for the wealthy and by the poor. The persons who gave their physical might in its construction still have not got any house to live in though they have made many structures like it. The persons who have bought the flats but not occupied them have probably many more such flats. The man who has put in the money probably owns many such buildings.

For the owner of the building it is his profession to make such buildings. For the architect too, it is a profession. And for the laborers also it is their profession to make such structures. All the three professions have their own mechanics and they have a dignity to defend. For the poor, their dignity lies in making money by the sweat of their brow. For the architect, the dignity lies in making use of his brain to make a beautiful and workable construction. The person with the money is proud to hold the strings of the purse for such constructions.

But who is the real builder. The money can buy the material but the material will lie on the ground without the labor. The architect can conceive but his ideas will remain on paper. The labor can do nothing without the money element. Even though all the three are equally responsible for the construction, the society calls the wealthy person with the money as the real builder. Our training of mind is such that we give greater credit to the moneyed people and minimal credit to the poor laborer. When any body asks the name of the builder we tend to name the purse holder as the builder. We never think for a moment about the architect or the poor laborers without whom the raising of the building was impossible. We never raise the toast to them nor we inscribe their names in the nameplates.

In the inauguration of many government buildings, it is the name of the government official or the politician that comes in the plaques. Never have I seen any mention of the poor laborers, though they sweated to make it possible. Why is this distortion in our thought process? Is it because they have no power and we respect only power, political or of wealth? It is a sad commentary on our thought patterns, the way we are trained to think and act in society. The poor laborers all their life build houses but remain without a house of their own. The society indeed treats them shabbily.

Our economic structure is such that money is the king. Those who contribute their life into the cause are only foot soldiers. The victory is credited to the king. The soldiers are only paid to buy their daily needs.

THE BUSINESS

Man has created many vocations out of selling nature
They dig the mountains and earth and sell the minerals
The sea is fished and pearled to make money
Even sand is removed from the river bed and sold
The water from streams and lakes is bottled
The air is separated and sold as oxygen and nitrogen

The forest is denuded for wood to become rich
The flowers, the fruits and many other products
Come in the market and people make money
The nature suffers for man and makes him rich

It is the business of man to plunder nature and rake in money
He digs for oil, gas and minerals
And runs his rails, cars and aircrafts

He adds his greed to his intelligence and calls it ingenuity
He moulds natural products and call it value addition
He kills animals for food and calls it game
He plunders nature and calls it business

He does not feel indebted to nature
But calls himself progressive
He has no gratitude to other species
And calls himself intelligent and superior
His inventions pollute and adventures kill
His love of himself, he calls his skill
His passion is money his success is pride
His profession is greed his method is deceit.

He is in the business of selling nature
Nature that provides resources for food and clothing

Nature that enables trade, industry and commerce
But gets in return pollution, and disfigurement
Would you call it a fair deal in business?

RELIGIOUS ACTIVITIES

RELIGIOUS FESTIVALS

Festivals are a time for rejoicing and religious festivals bring cheer and joy to all faithful. The timing of the religious festivals generally coincide with harvest sowing, cutting or reaping the fruit of labor. The stories, myths or otherwise are woven round some gods to bring a reason for joy and celebration. I am not the one to vouch for the truth behind these myths for they relate to periods so far away in time that no body knows the truth for sure. But one thing has always bothered me. It is to know whether there is a spiritual significance to these festivals or they are merely to rejoice and celebrate. I have a lurking suspicion that there is a spiritual significance attached to these festivals.

To me it appears that the periodicity of these festivals is such that we are reminded to renew our spiritual background from time to time in order to live a life of religion and ethics. These are occasions to remember God and do meditation in order to give spiritual diet to our soul. In our enthusiasm to live a life of work and enjoyment we are prone to forget our spiritual duties. These are occasions to remind us that we have another side to our life when we have to go inward and seek the blessings of the supreme power, which created us and is sustaining us through thick and thin. These are occasions to thank the lord and pray for His continued support.

In life we need many things; wealth, health, wisdom and power against evil. The festivals are an occasion to reflect and seek the blessings of the lord that concerns the specific need of our life. On Dussehra we seek power to defeat evil, on Diwali we need the blessings of the goddess of wealth, on Holi we want to forget the problems of life and rejoice freedom and brotherhood. Religious festivals are an occasion for community feeling, self-assessment, introspection and meditation. It is a time to renew vows of ethics and morality. In community celebration, it is a time to listen to the advice of sages, to follow the examples of the great religious leaders and pay respect to the powers that control our life. It is a time to feel oneness with nature, consider every living being as an image of God and experience the brotherhood of mankind. It is an occasion to see the light of God in the heart of every one, to show kindness to the weak and the poor and seek the blessings of the Almighty.

In our eagerness to enjoy the festivities, we often forget the real spirit behind the occasion. To celebrate the Navarattras, the nine-day worship of the nine manifestations of the goddess Durga, we forget the devotional aspect and spend all the time in enjoyment of music and drama. But the festival that comes twice a year is a reminder to us to meditate on the various manifestations of the creative spirit that is all around us. The occasion is for fasting and meditation and not for indulgence. The religious festivals are for celebrating the creativity of the supreme spirit in joyous mood. But the joy should not extend to indulgence. We must meditate on the blissful nature of the Reality, the ever-joyous supreme spirit, and seek the blessings and grace of that spirit in gratitude and reverence. It is not desired to turn the celebration into a noisy, loud or frivolous occasion with unspiritual acts..

OFFERINGS TO GOD

It is a very old practice in some religions to offer animal sacrifices to God. In case of idol worship, there is a practice of offering flowers, fruits, sweets and ornaments to the idol for pleasing the god of idol and seeking favors from him. It is indeed strange that the God who is almighty and the creator of universe should be pleased with such insignificant items. Generally, the argument given for such practices is that the offering indeed is to express one's love and gratitude to God. Further it is emphasized that such gestures are symbolic and God indeed is not in need of any of the things offered.

By such acts we try to translate our worldly actions in the realm of the divine. This indeed is strange if we know the nature of God. One who is omnipresent and omniscient hardly needs such gestures on our part to get pleased. I think what really matters is to act spiritually and pray with a feeling of unity with Him. Knowing His omnipresent nature, it would be much wiser to silently meditate on Him and offer all our actions to that supreme reality. This is what lord Krishna advises in the Bhagwadgita. There is no better offering to God than spiritualizing our thought, word and deed since He is the creator and knower of all.

As is generally known, there are two components of any religion. One is the internal, which is practiced through meditation and self-knowledge and the other is the external one in which ritual is performed.

Offering man-made items to God is merely a ritual that is so easy to perform. Meditation and self-understanding is rather difficult for it requires a mental effort. Doing things with hand is so mechanical and easy to do without involving any mental control. Moreover, the quantum of offering displays the devotee's wealth and status. The priests also prefer this outwardly action for it enriches them considerably.

One thing that is in favor of this practice is the prospect of business that flourishes with the spread of this ritual. The greater the number of items that are offered, the greater is the benefit to business. The greater is the quantum of offerings, the greater the profit. The society does indeed find ways to improve financial aspect in their dealings. The ritualistic practice offers employment to many. This is one way the God helps to sustain people. Who would object to this practice on this count? Religion is indeed bound with the lives of people and benefits them in many ways.

Generally we offer only those things that we like to have in our own life. The eatables, the cloth, the ornaments are all things that are part of our life. In eatables too we offer those items that we like most. The non-vegetarians would like to offer sacrifice of animals while the vegetarians would like to avoid it. Our choice of fruits and sweets is also dependent on our own likings.

It is however to be noted that scriptures have said that God is pleased even with a cup of water. And even when water is not there, one can simply remember Him and the person will have the fruit of many offerings. I think people have forgotten this basic fact. Commercialism seems to have taken over the practice of religion.

PRAYER AND WORSHIP

People all over the world pray to God, or gods, for health, wealth and peace. Every one encounters difficult days some time in one's life when appeal to the Almighty becomes necessary. Though in spiritual terms asking worldly things from God is not strictly the right way to practice religion, people do flock to places of worship for selfish ends. It is the practical side of religion that cannot be ignored. In spiritual terms, the right way to prayer is to ask the love of God and all the best for every one. But this is rarely put in practice. We need God to solve our difficulties because we feel helpless at times when solution to the problem eludes us. God is the savior and provider and we beg His favor to ride over difficult times.

Do only the weak pray? I do not think so. Every one comes across moments in life when one wants to pray. It is one way to autosuggest and use the power of subconscious to create conditions for the solution of problem. Subconscious has great influence on the thought patterns. It is the thought that ultimately drives you to achieve what you want to have. It is rightly said that you are what you think. Prayer is a means of influencing your motive power. It drives you to accomplish your desires. God works through your own motive power. If you regularly think of something, you unconsciously move to achieve that thought in practice.

The power of prayer is even recognized by psychologists, for it directly affects your thoughts. The answer to prayer lies within you. You may look it in another way, you pray to God and God resides within you. Therefore you are in fact praying to something that is within you. The answer therefore must come from within you. From spiritualists' point of view, it is the divine spirit within you that is omnipotent and omniscient. That spirit when addressed has the power to make you achieve your goal. It gives you the desired strength and direction to move to have your way.

The only condition for getting your prayer answered is to have a clear conscience and a pure heart. When you address your wish to the spirit within you, the contact is made only when you have a pure thought pattern. If your thoughts are cluttered with negativity, the prayer loses its effectiveness. In spiritual terms it is explained by the assertion that your soul, which is a part of the universal spirit, is surrounded by layers of negativity that you have entertained in your worldly interactions. When you try to address your prayer to that spirit, the negativity blocks your way to that divine spirit. It is therefore necessary that you clean up your actions to reach that divine presence within you.

The same applies to worship. Your worship is effective only if your thoughts are pure and your heart is clean. Otherwise it is a waste of effort. God within you is reachable if the surrounding negativity is removed by pious actions. The spiritual practices are meant to remove this surrounding negativity by adhering to universal values of truth, love and compassion and developing a pure life of divine existence. Prayer and worship are tools to address the divine within you. That divine is Almighty, omnipresent and omniscient, and capable of making you face any difficulty with inner strength. There is no magic in praying. It is your own inner strength of the divine within you.

RECITATION OF DIVINE NAMES

Recitation of *mantras,* the divine names, is a spiritual activity that helps in meditation. This helps in concentrating the mind on divine aspect of the supreme spirit, away from the mundane thoughts. In meditation, the senses are withdrawn inwards and the empty mind tries to run in every day thoughts about our desires, and relationships. To keep it focused on one point, the names of God are recited so that it does not waver from thought to thought. It is a simple technique to control the random movement of thoughts.

The recitation can be loud or silent. It is said in the scriptures, however, that silent recitation is thousand times more effective than loud recitation. The reason behind this statement is that when you are reciting loudly, the sound can distract you and move your mind to other thoughts. When you silently recite, your senses remain inward without any external distraction.

Theoretically, any name can do the job. But in practice, if you take the name of God, your thought remains on the divine spirit within you, which is your true nature. The purity of thought remains intact and your effort is confined to reach and make contact with the divine spirit. The technique is known by the name *Japa Yoga.*, the recitation technique to connect with the divine. The effectiveness of *Japa Yoga* is well established in the scriptures. It has been cited as a technique suitable for most people who find it difficult to concentrate on the abstract form (the n*iraka*r form) of God. The alternatives forms for concentration are a point, a flame, or any symbol like Om or simply an image that one likes most. The names of God that are used in *Japa Yoga* are generally the adjectives that assign certain qualities to God, though in fact the *nirakar* aspect of God is beyond any qualities.

Japa yoga is an aid to self-realization because the ultimate goal is to realize the true nature of self. In the long run the recitation leads to the realization that the same spirit pervades in the whole universe as in the multiple objects. The dual existence of pure spirit and its manifestations is in fact an erroneous impression of the senses. The ultimate reality is only the creative spirit that manifests as transitory objects in space-time domain. *Japa Yoga* keeps the mind centered on that reality.

In the traditional *Japa Yoga* technique, the names for recitation are given by the guru, the spiritual teacher. This is done in confidence and secrecy. The person is advised to repeat the words while concentrating on the divine spirit. The person is told to do it in silence in sitting or lying position in a calm and tension free environment.. Some persons prefer to use a rosary to facilitate the counting of a certain number of recitations.

Some persons keep reciting the names while doing other jobs. This is, in my view, hardly desirable since then the attention gets diverted and concentration is flawed. If you want to achieve the desired result, it is better to do it the right way. There are some *mantras* that are mentioned in *Puranas* and are prescribed for those who do not have any guru. Their potency depends on the spirit with which you recite them.

COMMUNITY SERVICE

It is well known that service to humanity is service to God. This is so because in every heart resides the same God that is within you. Service to humanity can be in many forms: healing the sick or the injured, feeding the poor, educating the illiterate, and helping the disabled in one form or another. Only a loving and compassionate heart can feel for the disadvantaged. The vulnerable sections of society, the children, the sick and old and the physically weak need help from the more fortunate ones. When you help the needy persons, you are doing the work for God because they form a part of His creation.

Many people think that helping the needy is a form of charity. A charitable work is considered a part of religious activity. They feed the people on festivals and religious functions. They arrange singing and dancing parties to celebrate religious occasions. They invite holy persons and *kathavachaks* for religious lectures and scriptural reading. They set up places for providing refrigerated water and other drinks on specific occasions. Some people plant shady trees and build resting places for weary travelers. They do all that for earning good points in the books of God. It makes them feel good and that is what matters. To the society they are the do-gooders who help the cause of community.

Every religion exhorts the people to help their fellow beings as a religious duty. In fact some religions even ask them to be kind to not only the humans but also all living beings. Some religious persons open hospitals and orphanages as a charitable activity. They make hospitals for birds and animals too. Feeding and relieving pain is a very noble activity especially for those sufferers who have no means to get such help. The benefactors get in return only the blessings from the unknown ones who get benefited from such charity.

Charitable work is not possible unless there is a feeling of love and compassion for all humanity. There are a number of schools and hospitals that run on charity. There are many religious institutions that operate schools and hospitals on a regular basis. The offerings made to big temples also provide finances for academic institutions and hospitals that are run through trusts. They supplement governments' effort to uplift the unfortunate ones to a better life. The charitable non-government institutions are an important component of community life.

Some people feel that charitable work can be done without involving religion in to it. This looks reasonable, but the involvement of religion can impart an important helping hand to this activity. In any working society there are persons who need the help of others since not all have the required resources at their command. However there is a caution for all such workers who engage in this sort of charitable work. They must not expect any thing in return as reward for then charity becomes a business. You may run charity with the efficiency of a business venture but not for profit. Any self-interest in charity work will nullify the good deed. As the Bhadwadgita says, do the work and forget the reward; then only you are a true karamyogi.

SATSANG—COMPANY OF THE HOLY AND THE WISE

Satsang is considered as one of the essential duties

of a religious person. The idea is to get the advice and wisdom from those who have traveled on the path to perfection. The religiously oriented person is advised in scriptures to have the company of the enlightened in order to share the knowledge and experience of the wise ones. In the company of the enlightened, the whole atmosphere is charged with religiosity. The religious company has lot of impact on the thought process of the seeker. The environment is calm and peaceful. There is discussion of religious topics, and from the speech of the wise one, one learns a lot about religious experience. Through the discourses, one moves on the path of wisdom. By joining the recitation of religious songs, one gets into the mood to concentrate on the supreme reality and one's devotional content improves.

By joining the company of religious people, one learns about the experiences of religious colleagues and tries to emulate the ways of the more experienced in religious matters. One becomes more understanding of the difficulties encountered in the spiritual path and how to get over the obstacles in the path to perfection. It is well known that company has a lot of effect on the making of a person; the shaping of character and shedding of the evil ways. One becomes loving towards the other devotees and tolerant towards the faults of others. By joining the group meditation, one progresses fast on the spiritual journey. The religious environment all around has a deep effect on the psyche of the person.

Though there are many advantages of keeping the company of the enlightened and the wise, it is also necessary to choose correctly the persons for company. It is important to be sure of the right credentials of the religious ones so that you gain by their company. The guru that you adopt should be a person who has attained the highest level of spiritual experience. The general criteria to judge a guru is that he or she must love and be compassionate, tolerant, learned, kind, sympathetic and knowledgeable of human temperaments. The guru should be able to judge you correctly so as to guide you on the path that is suitable for your temperament. He should not be money-minded or critical of the faults of others. He should radiate saintliness and spirituality. By this I mean he must have a good experience of meditation and should be able to cultivate the spiritual values in you.

In the spiritual arena, there are many who themselves have not reached the height of spirituality but claim to guide others in the path. Such half-baked gurus can hardly induce any spiritual experience in you. It is not advisable to go on the words of others to judge a good guru. One must oneself get convinced about the capability of the guru to take you to the pinnacle of spiritual experience. Unfortunately, the spiritual field is infested with false claimants and self proclaimed spiritual masters who lead others nowhere. A true guru will never demand anything from you. He will be full of the love of God to share that love with you. In this age of commercialism, it is important to be aware of the false gurus. Satsang is a religious activity that needs to be exercised with care. An undesirable company can harm to no end.

MEDITATION

Meditation is the oldest technique of self-realization. It is the essence of religious practice. All religions talk of concentrating on God and meditation is the technique to do so. Buddha invented his own method of concentrating by focusing attention on the coming and going of breath. Patanjali wrote a treatise on the methods and techniques of meditation. All those who speak of inner vision and realization of the inner world of reality talk of meditation as the means to achieve it. Spirituality and meditation are inseparable. Whatever means we may adopt, meditation is the only way to realize the self and reach the state of God-realization.

Even in *sakar bhakti*, meditation plays its role. From concentrating on the image of idol, the transition to *nirakar* happens when deep concentration brings the equality of all in the image of God. One then sees God in every being. It is meditation that brings this realization, the knowledge of self, as the omnipresent spirit. It is this spirit that is manifested in all-material beings. Meditation takes one to the state of no-mind, the thoughtless state of *Turiya* where one finds oneself conscious of just being.

Meditation forms part of *Ashtang* yoga, the eightfold path, of Patajali. In this the first two are concerning the ethics of personal and social conduct. The third is the taking of the comfortable posture for long hours of sitting in meditation. It should be at a place that is isolated from noise and pollution. The fourth is the *pranayam*, the control of breath. This exercise is done to stabilize the thoughts and purify the inner being. The fifth is the withdrawing of senses and shutting off the interaction with the outside world. Normally this is done by closing the eyes and blocking the ears so that external inputs of light and sound do not disturb the attention. The sixth is the concentration on any object that attracts you and fixing the attention on that. It is done so that thought does not waver. The seventh is the meditation, which involves uninterrupted attention on the object of concentration. This could be five minutes or fifty minutes depending on the practice. The object of concentration could be a spot of red color, flame from a candle or similar device, an image of an idol or simply an object or image of something that one likes most. The yogis prefer the spot, the flame or the symbol Om while for the devotees the image of their idle serves the purpose. The eighth stage is the state of *samadhi,* the state in which one goes into a thoughtless state for long uninterrupted hours becoming totally unaware of the surroundings. In samadhi one becomes inwardly aware of the pure consciousness, the universal awareness of the spirit that is the reality of being.

One may well ask why go to such a length to focus long hours of attention on an object. The answer to that lies in the fact that this meditative state de-stresses and brings many medical benefits to the person. It improves concentration, relaxes the person and improves the intuitive power of the meditator. It is a method to know the reality of one's self, the creative power that creates and runs the universe.

Meditation is known to do lot of good both spiritually and medically. It de-stresses and relaxes the brain, improves concentration and intuitive power. It opens the inner vista.

THE SACRIFICIAL FIRE CEREMONY

The sacrificial fire ceremony is performed on many occasions as part of religious duty. It is an age-old practice dating as far back as the Vedic times. Gods are invoked and sacrificial offerings are made. In some cases, particularly those that do not believe in image worship, it is a daily ritual. In the busy and stressful life of modern age, it is however becoming impractical to do it every day. Moreover, in view of ecological considerations resulting in ban on cutting trees, the availability of wood for burning is becoming scarce. But the belief that sacrificial fires purify the air persists. I am not sure how far this belief is valid on scientific terms.

The practice is related to fire worship that was prevalent as part of religious ceremony in Vedic times. The diehards are keeping it alive on the presumption that this invokes gods' pleasure. In the olden days, the availability of wood was no problem and keeping the fire burning was almost a necessity. But in the present context, I wonder if it is relevant to the practice of religion.

The best part of this fire ceremony is the chanting of mantras. Though the mantras are meant to invoke the gods, their relevance remains applicable even today, for they show devotion and respect to the nature's forces and advise universal brotherhood. The mantras make us feel the importance of ethical life and exhort us to lead a peaceful and socially relevant life.

There are many alternatives to this kind of religious practice. Meditation is the best option. Recitation of Gayatri mantra is another. But the faith in the celebratory fire worship is still intact. For every religious function, the sacrificial fire is considered a must. The ready-made items for performing this fire ritual are easily available on commercial lines and most people feel good if they perform this ritual regularly. All marriages, birthdays, naming ceremonies and other religious events have this fire ritual as an important part of the function. The event is not considered complete without the fire ceremony. In Hindu marriages, unless the couple takes seven rounds of the burning fire, the marriage is not considered complete, .

The abiding faith in the fire ritual is the essential element of Hindu religious functions. Vedic hymns are recited and offerings are made to the fire god. The important element in such functions is the coming together of the whole family in performing this ritual. Fire is considered the purifying element for the environment and the household. Oaths taken in the presence of fire as a witness are considered sacred.

The fire ritual is repeated in seasonal ceremonies as well. Seasonal festivals that include the fire ritual mark the end of winter and the end of rainy season. Many mythical tales are connected with this fire ceremony. All auspicious occasions generally have the fire ritual as an inclusive component. The traditional fire worship continues in one form or another in this ritual.

FASTING

In religious practice, fasting plays an important part. This is common in more than one religion. It is believed that fasting purifies the person and makes him eligible for God's grace. There are many religious festivals, such as *Janamashtami*, the birthday of lord Krishna, when people fast and celebrate the festival. It is one form of penance that people willingly go through in the name of God or gods.

Fasting is good otherwise too. For general health reasons, people like to observe fast occasionally in order to give some rest to their stomach. I have personally found that fasting one day a week is good for health. When I say fast, I mean avoiding the regular meals and taking only some fruit or milk instead. Some people take it to extreme where they avoid even water and observe silence too.

Fasting seems to strengthen the determination and improve strength of character since it requires self-control to a high degree. Not all people can succeed in remaining hungry for long. There are various degrees of fasting. Some do it for twelve hours; others for twenty-four hours while some can go for weeks. Medically speaking, the system responds differently for different people. There occur physical changes as the time of fasting is increased. If done indiscriminately for long periods, fasting can harm too.

Some persons, to put pressure on the authorities as a nonviolent opposition to government working, have also resorted to fasting. Gandhi used it to great advantage. It is still used as a mode of protest in nonviolent struggle.

There some persons who make a mockery of fasting by either eating too much before fasting or eat alternatives to cereals and feel satisfied that they have fasted. By doing this, they defeat the very purpose of fasting. There are some who fast for totally nonreligious functions such as weight reduction. They fast under medical advice or under supervision of dieticians in order to achieve their objective.

I do not know why fasting is given the religious color. But whatever the reason, it serves a good purpose. May be, the reason is that a healthy body is essential to move on the journey to self-realization. If your thoughts are centered on food and taste, you are hardly in a state to concentrate on higher objectives.

For some persons, enjoying food is a weakness that is difficult to resist. This is one indulgence that people do not include in the category of human vices. But preoccupation with thoughts on food and allied subjects make them lose interest in other intellectual pursuits. I have no hesitation in saying that man does not live by bread alone. He has many other priorities in life that make him soar to great heights.

Fasting also makes a person realize the unfortunate plight of those who cannot for various reasons afford to buy food. This should make them share their resources with such unfortunate ones.

THE SEARCH

I sought God in the company of holy men
But he eluded me
I searched Him in the temples
But idols looked blank at me
I offered the choicest gifts to him through the priest
But He did not acknowledge
I prayed and recited the mantras in praise of Him
But he still did not respond to me
I lit the sacrificial fire and meditated on Him
But he did not appear before me
I fasted myself and fed the poor
But He ignored me

One day in my utter frustration
I closed my eyes and ears
And looked within to address Him
In a tone of displeasure I asked Him
Why He so blatantly disguised

And refused to speak to me

Rather reluctantly, He spoke through my conscience
And said. 'You want to see me as an individual
Sitting in heaven and disbursing justice;
But you forget that I am limitless
And am present in all my creation.

Why don't you look for me,
In the blooming of a flower, in the thunder of storm,
In the gurgle of a stream, in the breaking of a wave,
In the colors of a rainbow, in the smile of a child,
In the wrinkles of the old, in the brightness of the youth,
In the hunger of the poor, in the affluence of the rich,
In the craftiness of the clever, in the intelligence of the scientist,
In the juice of the fruit and in the salt of the sea?
I am so commonly available and yet you do not see,
Does the fault lie in me or in your method of looking?
I make myself available in the heart of every one
But you look outward and ignore my presence within you.
I am present in every atom of my creation
You have only to reorient your sight in the proper direction
And you will find me, as you want to see me.
You must first know my nature and yours too
Before you start searching me
I am not elusive, only you ignore me.'

WHAT SHOULD I ASK?

It was a cloudless night. The stars were shining bright in the absence of moonlight. A day before, the rain had precipitated the dust and there was clarity of vision if you had the light. The foliage was thick and well-grown trees added to the darkness all around. I was sitting on the steps of a small village temple a few yards away from the rivulet that flowed nearby. The gentle evening breeze created the perfect environment for reflection. The evening prayers were in progress at the temple. A small gathering of villagers added to the religious fervor in the temple. It looked as if God had descended at the place and had decided to bless the devotees.

I was lost in my thoughts when suddenly I was jolted by a person who was leaving the place after the prayers. To avoid the embarrassment of colliding with me, he said in anger, 'what a place to sit. Why can't you be in the temple to pray and seek the blessings of the lord? Don't you have anything to ask from Him?'

I said I was sorry to have caused him inconvenience but I had no idea that a person would be crossing my path. As to the prayers in the temple and myself asking from God some goodies in boon, I said,' I hope you have got from God what you wanted. As far as I am concerned, I never ask anything for myself alone. Whenever I pray, I pray for all. This is what our Upanishads teach us. They always insist on asking peace and prosperity for all humanity. This stands to reason because all include the seeker too. The seeker is never in isolation from the rest of humanity. At least, this is the view of the Upanishads, which treat the whole world as one big family. Moreover, why ask the God in the idol when He is also present in our hearts. If at all I need any thing specific for myself, I would address the God in me to fulfill my desire. The God in temple is for those who have neglected the God in them. They search outside and find Him in temples or other holy places where they go for pilgrimage. I enjoy His presence within me and never find Him away from me. For me He is so handy. Whenever I need Him, I close my eyes and ears and talk to Him in silence. To me He speaks through my conscience. I listen to Him and act accordingly. I believe, you should also try this and establish a rapport with Him. He is kind to all and responds through your conscience. The condition is that you must first clear your conscience by shedding all negativity and live according to the universal code of conduct that includes truthfulness, love, compassion, brotherhood and concern for all. Even if you do not go to temple, God knows you well for He is omniscient. He will never miss your prayer, for He is present within you all the time that you spend in this life. Any way, here sitting on the steps, I am enjoying the peace and tranquility under the smiling stars and the cool breeze makes me grateful to Him. He has given me so much by way of happiness and contentment that I have no reason to trouble Him with any more requests. He has given me enough to fulfill all my needs and if I ask more, it will amount to sheer greed and ingratitude.'

What I said seemed to annoy the man and he said, 'you seem to be one of those infidels that disbelieve in idol worship. You do not seem to appreciate the power of faith. You must know that not every one can concentrate on God within. Places of worship play an important role in the practice of religion. There is an atmosphere of reverence and faith in such places, which immediately touches the person, and he bows to God out of love and respect. By frequenting such places you develop a habit of thinking of the divine power that affects you in so many ways. Intellectual reasoning against idol worship impresses only intellectually. But religion is a matter of faith and love for God. Intellect does not enter into it. So next time when you give your advice to a believer, think of my words.'

It was a retort that was partly right and partly wrong. It was not right to think of me as an infidel. He obviously missed my belief in God. But he was right in defending the role of the places of worship in religion. It is accepted world over. But not all are convinced about the presence of God within. Most people think of Him residing in heaven, and some believe Him to be present in the idols and listening to them. It is a matter of faith. . .

LIVING A VIRTUOUS LIFE

I was once attending the funeral of the relative of an acquaintance. The persons gathered there created an atmosphere of sadness and every body seemed to be concerned of the remaining years of their own. This is an occasion when most people turn philosophical about life and weigh their actions in terms of good and bad deeds. It dawns on them that they too one day will meet their fate. Consequently they become nervous about their past activities and want to lessen their tension by indulging in talk of life after death. If you are an observer and become attentive to their talk, you can feel their nervousness in their whispers about the shortness of life, about the need to do well, about discharging one's duties and the imperative of being on the right side of God. One would talk of earning *punya* (the reward of right action) while another would comment on the short life span and the need to do good actions to escape the wrath of God. Some would advise to remember God while others would wonder what happens after life. Some would look wiser and talk of Bhagwadgita and the philosophy discussed therein and emphasize the need to think and do right in life. But all of them, after the funeral is over, would go back to their old ways of living their life; a life to acquire and hoard, a life of grabbing, a life of pleasure and pain. The atmosphere of the funeral gives us all a momentary glimpse of the futility of life, a transitory experience of the sorrows that plague our life, a moment to reflect and be concerned about the nature of our actions, an occasion to be serious about the purpose of our existence and the roles that fate assigns us in this drama of life.

After a few days, as part of the concluding ceremony, I attended the prayer meeting in which all the relatives of the departed one participated. As is the custom, in this meeting a close relative or a dear friend speaks about the life of the deceased person. It is a summing up of the person's life and is supposed to bring out the good points of his career and personal life. Here too, a person stood up and eulogized the life of the deceased, stating that the person was a very virtuous person and looked after his family with love and care. His moral and ethical virtues were extolled with lot of emphasis and praised sky high. However, we all knew that in fact his life was a mix of virtue and wickedness as is the case with most of us. But since it is customary not to speak ill of the departed ones., we all gulped down the praise in deference to tradition. We have to be practical in life, living moments of truthfulness punctuated by untruth, cheating and grabbing with intervals of generosity and donation, helping and deceiving and such other acts of duality as suit our purpose of survival and self interest. This is the way of the world. To be virtuous all one's life is not easy. Most people are not prepared for a self-sacrificing life in the interest of virtue and truthfulness. They want to extract maximum pleasure out of their life. A life of virtue is a life of discipline and control. It is a life of spiritual awareness, and most people are neither concerned nor care about it. To them, life means an opportunity to enjoy and make the most of what they have. To live a virtuous life, it means to most people, exercising a great control over the desires, emotions and feelings, which they are hardly ready to accept. Even if some try to do so, the practicality of every day life puts a hundred and one obstacles on the way.

Leading a virtuous life has much to do with our belief in religiosity or humanism, depending on the way we have been brought up or have acquired wisdom on our own. A virtuous person may not be spiritual but a spiritual person is most likely to be virtuous. Without virtue, it is difficult to be spiritual though virtue can be developed without being religious or spiritually oriented.

In human civilizations around the world, the cultures may vary and the average intellect may change, but there is, in general, a commonality in the human failings, emotions and the feelings. People do feel concerned about goodness and evil in society. They are aware of the purity of heart, the helping attitude and the frankness of the people as against cunning, deceit and betrayal. Even in the most backward civilizations, people can distinguish between truth and untruth, love and hatred, and kindness and cruelty. Most people intuitively know the intent of others, though out of modesty, compulsion or fear they may not make it apparent.

They know the difference between the bully and the brave, the sycophant and the truly helpful, the caring and the neglectful and so on. Virtue is always visible, though at times we tend to ignore it out of malice.

A virtuous or a morally right person will have frankness about his conduct, even though it may cause difficulty to him personally. He stands for moral correctness, truthfulness and frankness in dealing with others. He is a person of valor, uprightness and chastity. His actions will avoid hurting others. He is a man of word, he says what he does and does what he says. His every action is justified on moral and ethical standards. Morally he is sound and ethically correct. Socially, he is balanced and even-tempered. Even when wanting in faith, he is just and spiritually alive. For a virtuous person, his virtue is his reward. He does not need social sanction for his deeds.

A virtuous man is committed to honesty and fair dealings. He keeps his promises and shies away from dishonoring his commitments. At times, a virtuous person may be seen as a soft target by the wicked. But it is wrong to see virtue as a sign of weakness. It takes a strong will to stick to virtue. A good-hearted person can be quite strong in his resolve to do right. The virtuous dislikes wickedness but not the wicked. He has an inborn love for humanity, a liking for the inherent goodness of man and a firm belief that in every heart resides the image of God. The true nature of every individual is full of love, compassion and kindness. It is the Karma and the circumstances that make a person forget what he truly is. It is the duty of every one to realize self and be in his true elements.

EXPRESSIONS

VEDIC TRUTH

Sometimes spiritual truth is expressed in a roundabout way. For example, the mystic saints like Kabir have expressed the deep spiritual truth of inner reality and how to reach that in very simple language that talks of ordinary daily events in our life. Understood in the ordinary sense there does not seem to be any spirituality associated with it. But when similes are seen in proper perspective, they represent deep spiritual truths. There lies the genius of the saints who express difficult concepts in such simple language that any one can benefit from that. Similarly, in Puranic literature, the concepts of Vedanta are presented in stories so that even a child can learn the message if a person can correlate the significance of characters and events properly. The sages who composed these stories knew the psychology of people whom they addressed. If religious truths are to be presented to largely uneducated people, they have to be addressed such that they relate theses truths to every day happenings in the life of the people.

What applies to the saintly language and Puranas also applies to the Vedas. Vedic language too describes events and happenings in nature that relate to people's life in intimate way. But seen in the light of spirituality, they represent truths that have deep influence on the spiritual growth of people. This however requires an insight of the interpreter into the essentials of spirituality to interpret the events correctly in the context of spiritual truths. The expressions of Upanishads are however more direct.

I want to illustrate the point with two examples. In the Vedas, the continuous tussle between Devas and Asuras is an indicator of the fight between good and bad intentions in our hearts that plagues us in most situations. The fight between Indra and Vritasur is symbolic of fight between good and evil. Love, compassion and concern for others are the characteristics of Devas while hatred, jealousy and self-interest is the mark of demons. The spiritual expression of truth, love and care is the theme of life of the good. The conflict between good and evil is eternal. It happens every day in our life. The spiritual literature expresses this in many ways and repeatedly tells us to be on the side of good.

The other example is the oft quoted churning of the sea by the gods and demons to get many things out of it, some good and others not so good. Here the churning of the sea is symbolic of the mind that has the depth of the sea. The means to churn it is the intellect. The Devas and the Asuras, gods and demons, are the good and bad thoughts that keep coming to mind. It is symbolic of the fact that through thoughts one can generate many ideas that can bring good and bad results, even elixir and poison, the immortality and painful life. The coming up of goddess of wealth and the god of medicine are symbolic of the fact that it is the mind that is involved in the generation of wealth and the development of the science of medicine. If the story is taken literally it sounds impractical. But the story is written with the purpose of making a point. You can bring health wealth and longevity through the churning of mind with your intellect.

I have given only two examples but there is any number of them in the whole spiritual literature to educate us in the art of living.

INTUITIVE EXPERIENCE

The expression of intuitive experience is quite complex and varied since it is person and subject oriented. To convey something to a person who has had no personal experience of that thing is difficult indeed. It is like tasting a fruit and trying to tell a person its taste when that person has had no knowledge of that fruit. The same applies when an enlightened person talks about his spiritual experience to an inexperienced one. The language applied may prove to be insufficient to convey the message correctly. Even facial and hand gestures may not prove to be useful enough. This is why expressing spiritual experience is so hard to explain in simple terms. Only faith comes to aid in the sense that a person believes what is being talked about. When faith is lacking and intellect revolts, it is next to impossible to understand the true state of spiritual experience. Further, the problem is confounded by the fact that this experience is subjective. Until the other person goes exactly in the same way to get that experience, it is very difficult to convey the exact nature of the experience. That is why the messages of the prophets and saints are prone to misinterpretation and misunderstanding by those whose mind is not in line with the thinking of the enlightened ones. This applies to the preaching by the interpreters too. But it is not so in the case of science or logic because then the language used by the teacher and the learner is the same. The same rules of logical thinking are used and there is unanimity on the grammar of the language used.

In view of the problem of likely misunderstanding in following scriptures or the sayings of the saints, the only course left is to inculcate faith in what is stated rather than argue about the validity of the statement. But then having faith without conviction creates its own problem of belief. The analytical minds may not like to believe what is not convincing to their intellect. They may need verification and evidence in support of the statement, which at times is difficult to provide unless the person goes through a strict regimen of spiritual practice. This creates the rift between believers and nonbelievers in matters of religion. We bypass the problem by bringing in faith.

The problem of interpretation of Vedas and Puranas, that too in a language not in current use in daily life, is indeed complex. At times it causes confusion and confrontation. But believing in the capability of the interpreter resolves this difficulty to a great extent. We believe the interpretation of scriptures by an authority like Shankara because we have great faith in his erudition and intelligence in matters spiritual. We believe he underwent the strict requirements of spiritual practice and consequent experience himself before enlightening others on the subject. Similarly we believe those western scholars who spent many years in learning Sanskrit and even became the disciples of modern saints like Raman Maharishi to first understand the meaning and then experience the teachings themselves before they presented that knowledge to the logical minds. It is the hard work of the interpreters that brings in the credibility of their messages to the uninitiated. Even then there are some diehard skeptics who remain unconvinced of the spiritual teachings because their sense mind is not tuned to intuitive thought. The translation of intuitive thought to sense mind is a difficult and specialized job that needs integrity of high order. If left to semiliterate persons, it can cause harm to the subject and the belief system to a great extent. No religion can afford to take it lightly.

In spirituality there is a world of difference between knowing a thing and experiencing it. Spiritual awakening comes from experience and not from mere reading about it. In spiritual practice lot of emphasis is placed in living the spiritual thought and not merely thinking or talking about it. The role of intellect in spirituality is limited to knowing or understanding the philosophical aspects. But experiencing the concept requires feeling the intense love of God and merging your whole personality in the divine love within. It is a matter of emotion rather than logical thought. That is why it is much more difficult for intellectuals to understand the devotional love for God. To them it may appear totally illogical to love an idol, knowing that the idol is incapable of returning that love. But to the devotees, the love of idol for them is as powerful as their love for the idol. In having spiritual experience it is necessary to shed all intellectual intentions of understanding God and submit totally to the divine grace.

Intellect in spirituality is needed up to a point, where the inquisitiveness about God is satisfied. Beyond that, intellect has no role in having spiritual experience. Beyond intellect, faith takes over. You cannot scientifically measure the intensity of love necessary to have the spiritual experience. It is a matter of feeling the presence of God within. The threshold of that feeling is subjective. For some it may be within reach of a few years while for others it may not come even in one lifetime. The ethical and moral state of the person is a factor relevant to this threshold.

Intuitive experience starts where logic of the sense mind ends. To mix the two is a grave error. This is made clear in the panchkoshi concept of the Upanishad. Intellect is used as a ladder in our ascent to spirituality in order to satisfy the queries about Reality and the divine role in our life. But having done so by the help of higher mind, or the Vivek, one has to leave the ladder of intellect and submit to the intuitive state of the higher consciousness. Intuitive state is the start of divine consciousness in the ascent to spiritual goal. Beyond this one enters into the universal consciousness and then into God-consciousness, which completely submerges the human will and the person acts according to the will of God. The transition from human will to divine will is the start of intuitive consciousness. This is the step where surrender to divine starts. In other words, this is the state of surrendering human ego to the will of God. At this point all human actions are for universal good and not personal benefit. All deeds are then for God and not for personal gain.

LOVE OF GOD

Most people want to be loved by God to get benefit from Him rather than love Him selflessly. The expression of love for God is generally through rituals. Rarely we find people loving Him out of religious sentiments or in silent meditation without seeking favors. People remember Him when they are in difficulties and when their worldly pursuits do not bear fruit. As one saint said, 'if you remember Him in good times, perhaps there would no bad times.' But we hardly listen to this advice.

Love of God is the first requirement for being a religious person. This love must express itself as the love for every living being, for He resides in all hearts. Love for God is synonymous with love for His creation. Those who distinguish between Him and His creation are ignorant of His true nature. Love of God for humans is more than that of humans for Him. But we like to think otherwise when we fall on bad times. We think that He has no time for us, ignoring the fact that He is present in every particle of our body. Our consciousness is a reflection of His universal consciousness. We eat, drink and breath what He created for us. Who would provide all the resources used by us unless He created these resources for our consumption? Those who deny His existence may call Him Nature, or the universal force, but the fact remains that there is a provider and we are the users.

Love of God increases as we progress in spirituality. This goes on improving till we merge in Him by shedding our individuality. Its intensity is a measure of our progress as a spiritual person. This love manifests in other forms of God as they too are in the image of the creator.

God is loved in different relationships, in different incarnations and different forms of affection. We love Him as father, the protector, as mother the caring one, the friend in need and as savior of all as the almighty. He has been loved as the spouse too as the saint Mira did.

Many saints have described God as the universal love personified as the love of Krishna. That love is for all, the saint or the sinner, man or woman, old and young, poor or rich. That love melts anger, hatred and jealousy and creates universal brotherhood among humanity. As many saints have pointed out, this love runs life on this planet and elsewhere. Without love of God, no existence is possible since He is existence, knowledge and bliss.

As Bhagwadgita says, one of the paths for enlightenment, the Bhakti path, rests on love for God. It is the easiest path and most suitable for the emotionally oriented devotees. It involves concentrating all emotional energy on the object of love, the incarnation of God. In this all intellectual doubts are set aside and pure love of the divine is the objective of life. The Leela of the lord is seen in the creation and as such the world becomes a playground of the almighty. We humans then become the players in His eternal play of life and death. The energy that sustains this play is the everlasting love of God

EXPRESSION IN INTERACTIVE WORLD

Ego is the main component of our mind that is responsible for our actions in the material world. Ego arises from our sense of individuality, as a body different from others. Our association with body is so strong that we refuse to think otherwise. We believe that we are what our body is. We keep it clean, and decorate it in many ways to impress others. Instinctively we act to protect it and act to feed it, and try to make it strong for survival. If it is not in shape we try all means to keep it healthy and well kept. This association with body is the cause of many faults such as greed, pride, unconcern towards others, and other selfish acts of every day life. Even in our close relationships, self-interest dominates. Our expression in the material world is thus completely body-oriented. Our mind too is mostly occupied with body-oriented thoughts.

Saints and mystics tell us that our preoccupation with body-centered living is not right. They tell us that our true nature is not body but the spirit within. Body-centered living makes us selfish, cruel, greedy, lusty, and makes us acquire traits that are not suitable for civilized living. Our false pride in us makes us look down upon others. We tend to be self-centered. As a result of this egoistic living, the society suffers. There is tension in society and we remain mostly tense and agitated. The peace and quiet of community suffers and we spend all our time in selfish pursuits.

The only way to reverse this trend is to look within and see the reality as it is and not as it appears. We must shift the focus from body-centered to spirit –centered. This shift moves us from individuality to universalism. We are part of the universal spirit that pervades in the universe and is the cause of creation. This shift in outlook at once removes our negative traits; that of working for self to identifying our self with the whole creation. This enlightenment of mind is the objective of spiritual practice. It sheds the egoistic expression to acceptance of universality as a way of life. Selfishness changes to universal good, greed to sharing, cruelty to compassion, and hatred to love. Since same spirit is seen in all, dislike for others loses its meaning.

When focus shifts from matter to spirit, the thought process finds a loving attitude towards all, for then every thing is seen as one's own. The concept of otherness loses its meaning. We find us reflected in all. To hurt other is like hurting self. This calms our agitation caused by individual interest and whatever we do, then we do for the good of others. Our expression of self is then one in all and all in one. Such an enlightened being is then nothing short of the image of God. The essential difference in man and God is in the scale of expression. God is infinite and eternal whereas man is finite and transitory. When the realization comes that man is a part of the same spirit that is infinite and eternal, the difference between man and man seems to fade away.

In the eyes of spiritualists, egoistic living is a sign of ignorance. To find the true nature of man through inner vision is the purpose of life. When thus enlightened, a person is lifted from mundane living to the divine level. Our true expression is spiritual and not material.

ATHEISM

Atheism appeals to those who are in denial mode to spiritual way of life. They deny the existence of a supreme power that we assign to God. According to them everything happens according to certain physical laws that are inherent in nature and there is no individual entity controlling them or overseeing them. There is nothing like destiny or preordained in nature. They strongly believe in the efficacy of prevailing circumstances, which affect the events. Cosmic events can be predicted according to the physical laws that govern the nature. Their belief in science is strong. They think extrasensory perception is a myth. Their reality is what their senses bring to them. The intuitive vision has no relevance in their world of belief. Paying obeisance to God is illogical to them. They go by logical reasoning and not by faith. Anything that is unsubstantiated by evidence has no existence for them. Their reality is matter and not spirit. For them religious rituals have no significance unless their efficacy is proved beyond doubt.

Atheism has existed along with religious belief for centuries. Much as religion has its followers, atheists have their following too. In a sense, atheism is also a belief system where you put your belief in the capacity of the senses to know the reality. Human senses, as we know from science, are not perfect. They see and hear only a part of the full spectrum of light and sound. The knowledge obtained by senses is therefore limited unless aided by other instruments. We supplement our senses with technology to increase our area of knowledge. The reliability of this data depends on the reliability of the instruments used.

Like the fundamentalists in religion, there are people among the atheists who refuse to accept the other viewpoint even when logical explanation is available. Their faith in the principles of science is so strong that they are unwilling to hear the arguments in favor of religious beliefs.

Like light and shadow, the belief in God goes along with disbelief in God. In this world of duality, it is quite expected that when you express belief in God, there will definitely be a person who goes against this belief. It happens in all classes of society, in all regions and all shades of religious beliefs.

The nonbelievers have the advantage that they are not burdened with concepts like heaven and hell, God's grace, sin, so on and so forth. They are totally free of any label of religion, rituals and myths connected with religions. They believe in their power to do right and do not blame God for their failures. They move ahead with self-confidence that a believer may lack. They make their own destiny and believe it so.

It goes to the credit of Hindu Philosophy that among the different philosophies of God, there is one, that of Charvak, that propounds atheism as a belief system. This line of thinking suggests the present materialistic philosophy of eat, drink and be merry without any burden of answering to God. For most people today, this seems to be the way of living..

LOOKING WITHIN

THE BUSY MODERN LIFE AND SPIRITUALITY

The present modern conditions of life are such that it becomes difficult to find time for spiritual pursuits. The competitiveness, the demands on time from family and the fast pace of technological changes makes it very difficult to sit quietly for contemplation and think of things other than material gain. The avenues for entertainment take whatever time is found between professional engagements. Most of professional and competitive activities are intellectual that agitate our mind and make us nervous. Rarely we sit serenely and bring poise in our life. Most of the time our mind and body are engaged in action of one kind or another. We hardly value the importance of passivity and stillness that is so important for the pursuit of spirituality. The modern society has no love for peaceful and noiseless life that values thoughtless inactivity.

Between the extremes of ceaseless activity and total stillness, there is need to strike a balance that enables us to do our duty and still find time for reflection. We need to have moments of silence after noisy engagements and stillness after feverish activity. This is necessary to rejuvenate our body and refresh our mind. We need to maintain the health of body and mind to tackle efficiently the problems of life.

Not only do we need to refresh our mind-body complex, we need to strengthen our soul too through practice of spirituality. This is done by reducing our external involvement and overcoming our material tendencies. We need to turn inwards spiritually to improve our present and future. But the demands of present society are such that it is becoming increasingly difficult to pursue the spiritual path. We are turning too intellect oriented and less intuitive. This is taking us away from our true nature that is intuitive and divine.

The materialist however disagrees with the need to develop spiritually, for he has no faith in the spiritual aspect of life. For him, the material gain and development of intellect are of paramount importance. He lives in the world of senses and for him sense satisfaction is the primary aim of life. He thinks that time spent in spiritual activity is an avoidable waste.

But saints and mystics have told us that time spent in meditation is not a waste but a desirable activity for gaining inner strength. They consider it as of vital significance. The mystic does not say that scientific temperament should be abandoned. On the contrary, he insists that one should personally test the efficacy of spiritual gain, through development of good conduct and practice of meditation. He is for the search of truth, whether by science or by intuitive thought. It is science that insists on material investigation and looks at mystic path as cranky and eccentric. The mystic investigation however, cannot be done in a laboratory. It requires a long effort on ones own person.

Some persons are fearful of the consequences of meditation. They think it will adversely affect their thought processes. But the mystic denies this fear and considers it a gift of God to man in order to realize his self and profit by it spiritually. All that is needed is to have an instructor, and sufficient determination, poise and patience to pursue the path. The result is a perfected man, a complete man with good health of body, mind and soul.

The presence and activity of soul eludes the brain. It cannot be realized without special training. In one view, we all are in search of our soul, some knowingly and some unknowingly.

According to Paul Brunton, the soul is perfectly knowable and experienceable. It is in our hearts and minds. The knowledge and experience of soul, once gained, lifts us into a higher plane of existence. It is for consideration why people devote their whole life in its pursuit, knowing it, experiencing it and making others do the same. It is quite astonishing to think why they do it when this soul is beyond sight, hearing, touch, smell and taste. It is interesting to note why people from times immemorial have been in this pursuit in religion and philosophy and why mysticism has intrigued people of all ages in all times. It is all done in the fond hope of having a divine life. It is perhaps the soul that drives him to that end. Man has an inner urge to seek the infinite and the eternal. The discovery of soul is a continuous and ever existing effort of man. It beckons him like a beacon of hope for a better life.

Much as there have been, and there will always be, nonbelievers in soul in any section of society, there have been, and there will be, seekers of soul, truth and divine life; howsoever they may be mocked at or ridiculed. If science is seeking the truth, it will inevitably seek the solution to this mystery of intuitive truth. It cannot postpone unearthing the truth of existence indefinitely. The part of man that lies dormant and waiting to bee explored cannot escape the attention of truth seekers.

The discovery of soul lies in the depths of mind. That can be reached through the systematic exercise of meditation and freeing of the mind from ceaseless thoughts. As clarity of vision comes in muddied water when it is still with mud settling down, so the mind needs to be quiet and free of agitation in order to make it see the reality. An agitated mind acts on the surface and depth of perception is dulled. The reality escapes us when we are enmeshed in worldly thoughts and preoccupied with sense inputs. A quiet, serene and still mind is necessary for inner vision.

To the mystics, this inner vision of reality is the higher purpose of life. Only in enlightened state a person finds himself free of doubts, satisfied in life and ever happy. It is the blissful state that sages talk of. The religious call this the divine or heavenly state of existence. It is the state of inner peace.

Before proceeding in this path a person must be clear what he wants to achieve through spiritual practice. Does he want religious satisfaction or metaphysical truth or moral power or inner peace or psychic faculties? Does he aim a theoretical understanding or does he want to do practice every day to realize self. His aim has to be clear to achieve his goal.

THE PATH

For the elderly, morning and evening walk is a part of life. It keeps the body healthy. In one such walk my friend once asked me what was so special about spirituality that people talk a lot about but few take it seriously enough to practice it in their life. I replied that it is about becoming a better person in thought and action and to realize the truth of one's existence. It is an age-old path that has been traversed by a few, who became enlightened and then showed the light to millions of others. It is about achieving perfection as a human being.

In the beginning of the quest for inner truth, the goal looks elusive, but keeping faith in the higher power drives one forward. In the end of course the realization comes that one was right in following the path. In the beginning, the person is instinctively drawn to the path. It is the intuition that takes him to the experience of it. The truth of existence lies buried in all of us. It is unknown and untouched.

The truth about higher power is realized either through the Guru, or God's grace or one's study and reflection. One can also keep pondering on the question of reality of self till the enlightenment dawns. It is not that God does not want to give us peace of mind. We remain disturbed only because our preferences in the world are different from the search of inner reality. In spiritual parlance the heaven and earth signify the peace of mind due to inner wisdom and mental agitations due to egoistic desires respectively. One must make a choice what one wants and move accordingly. This is reason enough for spiritual quest. To speak to God it is necessary to listen to him by going inward. Further, it is for consideration whether man, after conquering the environment outside, should conquer the inner self too.

The difficulties encountered in moving on the path of self-realization should not discourage us to take the first step. There is no point in hesitating or waiting to make the journey. It is also not necessary to see the end of journey. What matters is moving on the path and make the progress. For, what we achieve stays with us and helps us to move ahead. Nothing goes waste in this venture. One must make this life useful for making the discovery of soul. The aim however must be to make this discovery in this very life and not postpone it to future. Saints and mystics have repeatedly affirmed that this is the purpose of our birth and we must fulfill it in this life.

One must question the purpose of birth and not rest with mere survival. Our intellect must help us to find the answer. When intellect fails, we must rely on the intuition and follow the inner voice. Not every one is satisfied with mere existence. A wise person keeps asking the question and deliberates on the paths to know the answer. If one is convinced about the path to follow, one must take steps to start the journey with faith and belief in oneself. One must not be deterred by either the obstacles or the length of journey.

Those who are unsatisfied with worldly achievements are the ones who desire the experience of inner reality. The futility of desires and emptiness in heart gives rise to the urge to discover the reality.

TEMPLE OF GOD

It was raining heavily. The tropical rain literally pours; if you happen to get caught in it you are bound to get drenched to the skin. In this weather I was enjoying the happenings outside. Some pulled out their umbrellas when forced by the need to get out, others ran for cover and some enjoyed the plight of others when rain made them wet. It is human nature to enjoy the difficult circumstances of others, for it gives them a feeling of safety over others. The street dogs crouched in their shelters. Only one man moved unconcerned of this rain; and that was my friend who came to see me but was caught unawares in this rain.

When he reached my abode, he greeted me and sat in the chair lying by my side. I offered him a hot cup of coffee which he thankfully drank and wiped himself dry. Then he asked me, 'do you intend to go to the temple tonight since there is a big function there with collective prayers and singing of devotional songs in praise of the lord?' To tease him, I said, 'are you sure God will be there tonight to listen to the devotees' pleadings? He may have other engagements which may be more pressing for Him.'

My friend laughed and said, ' I know you do not view God the same way as others do. But even your infinite and eternal God is likely to be their, for he is present every where at all times.'

'But then why must we go to temple to have His blessings? Why can't we talk to Him at our place, particularly when the weather is not so favorable? Isn't He omnipresent and omniscient? You and other devotees want to isolate Him as an object for worship, distinct from other objects of the world, which is in direct contradiction to his omnipresence and omniscience. Why must He choose to be present in the temple exclusively as an observer to your doings?'

'I know God is present in every atom of the material universe as the force that binds the atom, as the force that binds atoms to the molecule and even as the force that runs the universe as per the universal laws, as the force that is behind all the laws of physics and chemistry, and even the laws of biological existence. But temple is the place where we condense all these ideas into one entity that commands our respect and devotion. Temple is one place that provides us the ambience and environment to concentrate our thoughts on that one entity and lose our individuality in the infinite existence we call God. It is difficult to do so in the presence of our worldly problems that beset us in our daily working conditions, the conditions that prevail in our households and office environment. You need to bring infinite to the finite in order that our three-dimensional brain may visualize and think of that one entity that we adore and pay respect to. Not every one can visualize the infinite and be in communion with the infinite and eternal. We need to devise ways to do so.'

'I agree with your statement on the need to have the proper environment to concentrate our thoughts on God. Temples, mosques, churches and synagogues serve that purpose. But to say that God specifically resides in these places is stretching the point too far. If you can create the environment elsewhere the need is equally fulfilled. Human heart is one such place. To conquer your mind, you do not need the space of temple or such other places. It can be done within the four walls that you call your home. Whoever is sensitive to the qualitative improvement of the environment and self takes the first step to spiritual development. On following the path of spirituality, one's aimless wanderings in lust and desires of the world ends, and a new and purposeful day dawns that frees one from all fears and doubts.'

'Man could be the temple of God, but without spirituality he is just a structure with no light and no purpose. In the search of soul, any help by way of creating a suitable environment is welcome. And temples and other places of worship fulfill that need. Besides this, you may come across in such places some persons who are more enlightened than you are. They may provide the trigger for you to start the journey to wards spiritual attainment. We may also experience the divine in their quiet company by silencing our emotions and intellect. Such enlightened persons shine like candles and attract seekers like the moths to a flame. One must also remember that the reality behind our attainments in arts and sciences is the spirit or the soul that by nature is beauty, truth and goodness. Attaining the knowledge of our true self is more valuable than the possession of material wealth. The quest is long and needs time to give results. It must therefore start early in life and not to be postponed till the graying of hair. It is wrong to say that heaven is beyond us and far away. We can all create heaven on this planet by our spiritual actions and divine thoughts. Violence, aggression, hostility, brutality, cruelty, and bloodshed are signs of the lack of spirituality in our thought, word and deed.'

'I was only trying to hear your philosophical ideas about localization of God. I do agree with you on the reality of God's existence among us. It is our limitation and not His that we fail to experience his presence in us. Let us all take the first step towards spiritual behavior by improving our conduct towards others.'

'Knowing that God is present everywhere and even in our hearts, we go to temples and worship the idol of God as if He is present among us as a living being. This dual presence surprises the intellect but not to the feelings of devotees who accept this duality as a fact. It strengthens their belief about

God as one living almighty who is helping them, seeing them and listening them. They pray to Him, plead to Him and talk to Him as if He was alive and listening to them. This is faith personified. Majority of Hindu faith survives on this mode of worship. The intellectuals may find faults with it but it is a living faith with the worshippers. I see no difficulty with it because religion is all about belief and faith.'

'I see your point. But religion is also about universalism and social conduct. The places of worship like temples and mosques are often centers of budding conflicts where differences in rituals create difficulties in the social structure. Most conflicts of violent nature emanate from such centers where mob thinking is manipulated by vested interests. Not all people who go to such places of worship are discerning enough to distinguish between right and wrong. They go by what is told to them in the name of God. I would personally prefer to remain at home and talk to my God within. It would be the best way of spiritualizing myself without in any way harming others.'

THE PREPARATION

'Is there any requirement to be met before embarking on the journey to self-discovery? Generally we find, when the journey is difficult and a long way to go, we need to prepare ourselves for the arduous path.'

'Yes, you are right. The journey to self-discovery is long and difficult with many obstacles on the way. Firstly, only a few have the strength and perseverance to start on the path. Secondly, one must be convinced of the necessity to embark on the journey. Spirituality is not for avoiding the temporary suffering. It requires strong desire to seek the truth. Mere curiosity about spiritual path is not enough to succeed in the pursuit. A determined action is also required. One must have the necessary will power to improve one's thoughts and actions. Therefore the third requirement is to change the thought patterns and personal conduct. One must develop love for all, and live a life according to the divine laws of existence with compassion and concern for all. Fourthly, one must be calm and patient under all provocations to the contrary. Slowing the pace of life helps a great deal in this pursuit. The last but not the least is the deep veneration for the higher power of the divine. Ego and arrogance arising out of self-importance are deterrent to progress in the path. In short this quest is for those who value mind over matter and spirit over mind. The running after material objects is the greatest obstacle in the growth of spirituality.'

'In this technological age of scientific development and material advancement, is it justified to opt for this esoteric belief and spend time for goals that are not very clear and uncertain to achieve?'

'Your doubt is justified because in this age majority of people expect to gain from science and very few have the mental courage to go for spiritual advancement. In this quest for self-discovery, people with good mind and good character can enter and hope to succeed. Sincerity, self-discipline, and sensitivity to intuition go a long way in assuring success. The place of humility in self-discovery cannot be under rated by the seeker. The humility here includes the knowledge of one's shortcomings and ignorance. Among the successful seekers are those who are capable of individual judgment and independent thinking. One must also remember that in this quest righteousness is not the only quality required. It needs compassion too, not outwardly displayed but inwardly developed for one and all.'

'With so many qualities required, it seems an uphill task to proceed in the spiritual path. Perhaps that is the reason why so few persons opt for this path. It seems you need to become near perfect before you claim any spiritual trait in your personality.'

'One need not despair, for whatever progress you make, it stays with you and you take over from that point onwards in this life or in later lives. Pessimism has no place in this pursuit. It is a path of inner wisdom and wisdom comes in time with consistent effort. It is well-trodden path by the early saints and mystics. They are the shining examples for the initiates. Divine grace comes to those who persevere.'

'Are there any more requirements for starting on spiritual path?'

'Yes, the seeker has to fight the temptations and desires of the material world and the societal traditions that block the path. The quest for inner peace is neither an emotional demand nor an intellectual exercise. It is a deep-rooted desire to understand and experience the reality of existence. Some come to spiritual practices for gaining occult powers but they remain on the surface and never penetrate the region of truth. The desire for inner peace arises in those who are tired of anxieties and problems of life. Even after material success they remain unsatisfied in life. They are the ones who adopt this path. But the objective cannot be achieved unless they attain self-control and self-improvement in thoughts and deeds. The egoistic cannot hope to succeed in this pursuit of peace.

The discovery of soul is a life long effort. Only the noble and the enquiring minds can hope to proceed smoothly in this difficult venture. Those who value the Truth are the right candidates to proceed towards success. The search for truth is for those who are prepared to kill the animal in them and seek the Divine. The object of seeking the truth is finding the answer to the question' what is the source of consciousness.' The same Divine that lies within helps the seeker in his search. It is indeed meaningless to attract others to this quest when they are unprepared for it. The desire to seek the Divine must come from their hearts. Those who have the will do find the way.'

'You seem to make a distinction between the right seekers and wrong ones. Is this justified? I believe, the path should be equally open to all.'

'The path is open to all. But the success is assured to those who have the will, the determination, and the right conduct to pursue the difficult task. Nothing is gained by trivializing the effort. There must be sincerity and deep desire to move on in spite of obstacles and temptations. Acceptance of one's ignorance and weaknesses is a sign that one is ready to shed ego and enter the domain of truth. Those who have found their life of materialism shallow and meaningless are ready to listen to the alternative.

It is not that common people are not evolving to spiritual goal. It is just that they will take more time to reach the goal than the spiritual aspirants who take the path with sincerity and conviction. It is an observation that most of the seekers are likely to come from the middle strata of society.

Further, there is no age specified for starting the spiritual journey, though earlier the better. In practice however, the persons in the middle age and elderly are more receptive to the ideas of spiritual experience. Probably, it is because they saw life and became disenchanted with it.

The path is not for the emotionally unbalanced nor is it for purely intellect-oriented who over rate their bookish or technical knowledge. Such persons do not have the patience or the humility to experience the divine.

The journey should not begin before getting prepared for it. The human qualities like love, compassion, serenity and calmness have to be developed in order to understand the implications of the chosen path. The path is also not for the untruthful, lazy, cynics and the prejudiced.'

WHO AM I

Science tells me that I am a creature of nature
That nature is ruled by some physical laws
Science gives me knowledge about planets, stars and galaxies
It informs me of the biological creations
About cells, proteins, DNA, tissues and bones
But it does not answer my question
What is the source of my consciousness and who am I?

The scriptures talk of their own versions of creation
Of physical bodies, animals and human beings
They talk of gross and subtle, living and nonliving
They inform me I am a child of God
That God runs the universe and my existence is an illusion

But they do not answer convincingly
What is the source of my consciousness and who am I?

I search for the answer here and there
I ask the wise. The intelligent, and the sacred
But I am not satisfied
An inner urge drives me forward
And I go inward
The light within silences me
And frees me from all queries and doubts

THE MULTIDIMENTIONAL ONE

The ant lives in 2D world
While we in 3D
What of the being that lives in higher dimensions?

The 3Dbeing is god to the 2Dbeing
Is not the multidimensional being a god for us?

The scriptures tell us there are more levels of existence
Higher than the one in which we live
Consciousness rises from the lowest (body) to the highest (divine)
They say the Divine is at the fifth or the seventh

We creatures of 3D are bound to the material plane
What if we rise to the plane of the Divine?
The urge to rise is the root of spirituality

THE IMMORTALITY OF THE MORTAL

It was the month of March, the middle of spring when the nature is in the mood to rejoice. Plants were getting buds, the trees welcoming the new leaves. Butterflies were happy to flutter over the flowers. Their colors competed with the colors of the flowers. The air was soaked with fragrance and animals, including humans felt the spring within them.

I was taking the evening stroll in a garden when I overheard a conversation between two persons who seemed to be oblivious of the nature around them since they were vehemently arguing about something. I felt curious to know the subject that attracted such energy in the discussion, particularly when it made them ignore the beautiful surrounding and produce only verbal out put with such vigor.

To satisfy my curiosity, I came nearer on a pretext and sat there to over hear their arguments. One was saying, ' how do you say that immortality to a mortal is of no consequence when we have this subject discussed in our Upanishad and Puranic scriptures with great importance. One of the main objects of self – realization is to attain immortality by being one with the infinite and eternal. Immortality is the carrot that is shown to all seekers of spiritual experience. The spiritual practices are meant to advance the span of life to eternity.'

The other said,' the immortality of some sages and gods looks to be mythical in view of the fact that that all matter eventually must cease to exist as matter and that it may change its form, size and shape in new incarnation only in the form of energy. All matter is essentially only vibration. The energy of vibration can and does change its form. The immortality of physical object, including human body, can therefore be talked only in terms of energy and not as matter.'

'But our Puranic literature is replete with tales of sages who lived long enough to be present in different eons of time. As an example, sage Vishwamitra appears in *Satyuga* as well as in *Tretayuga*. Is it not near immortality of the physical being?'

' I am sorry, but such mythical tales and characters are taken on faith and cannot be the subject of argument. Either two different persons may be having the same name or the character is mythical in the tale. Any way there is no point in discussing faith since it is a touchy subject.

Immortality in Upanishads is that of spiritual plane and not that of the physical one. The person is expected to live after death in the plane of the spirit. The doings of the material plane are carried over to the subtle existence in the spiritual plane.

The sages talked of eternity in the sense of living in the present always and not be in the past or future. The immortality of living being was equated to the immortality of the soul and not that of the physical body. They did realize the transitory nature of matter. Once a person reached the divine level of existence he/she entered the domain of soul's merger with the Absolute. At this merger the person loses the identity as an individual and becomes one with the Universal. He/she becomes one with the spiritual reality that is infinite and eternal.'

This explanation looked reasonable to me since I too fancied the human immortality to be that of soul and not the physical body. It is repeatedly asserted in the Upanishads that immortality applies to the subtle existence in the divine plane and not to the material body. The physical body is perishable and is incapable of eternal existence. All matter in the universe perishes with time and science attests this truth. The material universe of planets, stars and galaxies has a finite life, though long by human scale of existence.

The reward of spiritual practices is to reach a state of merger with the infinite and eternal in the spiritual plane. The material existence is transitory. It is immortal in the sense of subtle form of soul, which transmigrates from one body to another. The matter is eternal in the sense of energy, which only changes form from one body to another. The eternal cycle between matter and energy goes on forever and is part of nature. There is indeed no point in clinging to one form of matter hoping it to remain forever. If one wants to be immortal, be one with the eternal in the spiritual plane, the reality of all existence...

What good is the strength if it is that of a mad elephant?
What good is the intellect if it is merely argumentative?
What good is the beauty if it is without character?

What good is immortality-
If one lives for oneself and has no concern for others,
If one's anger is uncontrolled and harms others,
If one snatches from others what rightly belongs to them,
If one's greed knows no bounds,
If one is tyrant and lords over others,
If one is lustful and unkind to the weak,
If love has not touched one's heart,
If one trusts no one,
If one is haughty, cruel and arrogant,

And has no respect for the Supreme?

That is why God gave knowledge but no immortality to man.

THE LIGHT WITHIN

(According to Vedanta school of thought, our real nature is Atman, the soul or the spirit within)

I am not the body, mind or the intellect
I am the light within
I am the source of consciousness
The power behind senses
As the Upanishad says, the eye of eye, the ear of the ear

I am the intuition, the discernment of mind,
The wisdom of the enlightened
The light of the stars, the laws of universe,
The power of the righteous

I am the conscience
The positivism of life
The answer to the prayer
The dispeller of ignorance
The bliss of the Yogi
The light of awareness

I am the energy of the atom
The knowledge of the humans
The silence of the vacuum

I am the light within and without
I am Atman, the soul, and the life of man
I am infinite and eternal

I am Existence, Consciousness, and Bliss

A PRAYER

God, make me
Honest, among the dishonest
Brave, among the cowards
Wealthy, to give charity
Strong, to help the weak
Wise, to avoid pitfalls
Intelligent, to understand the world
Spiritual, to see the light within
Sincere, to my friends
Faithful, to my companions
Obedient to my seniors
Kind to my juniors
Loving to my relations
And compassionate to the suffering.

DUALITY IN LIFE

So long as we live in this physical world and lead a material life, the dualities of pain and pleasure, health and sickness, wealth and poverty, and happiness and sorrows are part of life. We cannot escape this duality because this is embedded in the very nature of material existence in the physical world. Every one is troubled by unpleasant happenings and one wishes that this did not happen in his/her life. But are sorrows of the world really unwelcome? Or do they serve any purpose? Is nature wrong in making us go through them? Is God unjust in treating us badly? In spiritual domain these painful events have a purpose and nature provides them for our spiritual growth.

It was a day of bright sunshine. But in the jungle in which I was going, the sun filtered through thick leaves and became weak and grayish dark by the time it touched the ground. Right through the jungle, a rivulet flowed making sounds as it past the stones. To the nature lovers, it was a sight to enjoy. But to the city dwellers that are at home with the crowds and noise of traffic, it was a dull, dreary and dreadful sight. I was enjoying my walk in this environment because I had opted to come here and enjoy the loneliness and fresh air of the jungle.

As I was moving along the side of the rivulet, a person wearing ochre colored clothes came and stood watching the water. After a few minutes, he removed his clothes and took a dip in the water. Then he came out and sat near the stream in a cross-legged position to meditate. I watched him with interest and waited for him to complete his meditation. After about half an hour when he started to leave, I asked him what brought him to this place and whether he came every day. He smilingly replied that he was a regular and that he enjoyed the environment, which was perfect for his daily ritual. Knowing that he was a holy man, I wanted to engage him in conversation to have some answers to my questions on spiritual life. I asked him,' why is it that in this world every human being has to suffer pain and pleasure? In fact not only pain and pleasure, we have to undergo so many aspects of duality like love and hate, honesty and dishonesty, goodness and evil and so on?

He calmly replied, 'I am not the fit person to reply to your questions because they concern the philosophers. However these questions concern my life too and therefore I will try to tell you what I feel about it. My reply may not satisfy you because you may not agree with the philosophy of Karma and other Vedanta thoughts.

I feel that duality is embedded in the material world. Good and bad are two sides of the same coin. It is not possible to get one and throw the other. Our mind gets incessant thoughts, both good and bad in the sense of the material world. The thoughts arise from our subconscious that has both types of karma related impressions in it. How we react to these thoughts depends on our training of mind. If we exercise our intellect and apply the filter of discernment, we act well. This makes our personality and in turns our Karma. . If we let our mind run its own way without discernment, we do both good and bad and we live to suffer and enjoy.

The duality lies in our mind. But if we live in pure consciousness, we live in pure bliss without sufferance. The scriptures tell us to rise above duality through self-realization. If you know the cause of sufferance you can take steps to overcome it. The way to do so is through spiritualization.'

This short discourse made my evening. I realized that spiritual way of life was the way to wisdom. The duality is in our external reactions to events. Our inner realization overcomes this perception. I thanked the person for his views and came back wiser.

THE SIGNIFICANCE OF SORROW

The state of shock arising out of extreme suffering and bereavement stills the mind in numbness in which one sees the reality of life. At that moment the material aspect of life loses its significance. The mind then moves to a state of observer, detaching oneself from the involvement of activity. The desires then lose their appeal. The utility of these black moments is that they give a sense of detachment, though forced by circumstances, an involvement in spirituality that borders on renunciation and a sense of futility of running around in the pursuit of material gains. Such moments for some persons open the door to the higher path. Most people complain of suffering, but a few take this more maturely as an initiation to the path of spirituality. These are the moments when ego dies and one is driven to reality of life. The desires, passions, greed and hates evaporate and one learns to live inward. The sorrows of life therefore are precious moments when inward reality comes forth and we expand our consciousness from the physical to the inner self.

It is not only the shock of bereavement but also the shock of unreasonableness on the part of others that can produce the same effect. The unfairness of treatment in job or deceit by the near and dear ones pushes a person to disappointment in worldly affairs. Such unexpected disappointments lead to disenchantment with life and one starts exploring alternatives to worldly living. In fact any crisis in life can result in a shocking situation. Defeat, failure, deceit and selfishness of loved ones can create the same effect leading the person to find success, peace and tranquility elsewhere away from his/her material engagements. The shock can drive a person to disillusionment of the attractions of life. There is resentment and indignation at the so-called material pleasures of life. A jarring feeling sets in that throws a person out of the circle of material life. A new look takes root and one gets attracted to spiritual thoughts that promise peace and harmony out of the rut of life. Such shocks uproot a person from the every day working life and one feels alone and lost to the world of activity. The world loses its meaning and the subtle domain of spirituality beckons. Some people end their lives while some return to get immersed in spiritual way of life. The new outlook in life makes them rise in esoteric experiences of spirituality. It is the breaking of heart that bonds with spiritual attractions.

Any shock of strong emotional upheaval is like a sudden arousal from the egoistic sleep to the spiritual awakening. It snaps the connection from the materialistic sleep and joins with a new state of existence. Most egoistic people need this jolt to enter the spiritual domain and break with old habits of attachment. Perhaps this is the way the nature acts to bring spirituality in one's life. This is an occasion when man likes to find the truth and purpose of life and asks questions about life, God and the relationship of man with God. The person begins to feel that there are higher powers and higher laws of life that are beyond one's comprehension. There arises an urge to understand them and experience the higher power.

One must remember that mysticism is not a religion but a quest for truth. This quest can start when one tires out from the material world and the transitory happiness of earthly possessions. It is a quest to find a meaning in life. It is an alternative presented to a person when material world fails him. When majority may find happiness in worldly achievements there are a few who find the world disappointing to their high ideals and it is they who start on the journey to explore and learn. They are the ones who embark on the journey to spiritual goal.

Even though a mental shock is one reason for turning some people towards spirituality, some other reasons for doing the same are as follows

Those who want to escape from the stresses and strains of material life

Intellectuals who want to explore the inner domain of existence, the truth of being

Those who feel that there are higher laws that govern life

Those who want to verify the existence of soul

Those who have an urge to listen to the mystics and follow their advice

Those who have a mental crisis and search for peace in the deeper recesses of their being

Those who are encouraged by the spontaneous

spiritual experience
Those who have a thirst for self improvement- a kind of superhuman revelation, an intuitive feeling
Those who are in search of unending happiness
Those who want to expand their consciousness to levels not reached in normal life
Those who are happy in material life but are inquisitive also about truth of existence- a kind of spiritual scientists who want to reach a higher plane of existence
Those who have an inner urge to go inward even at the cost of one's pride, ego and the will to lead a safe, stable and prosperous life. Buddha belonged to this category.
Those who renounce the meaningless existence and withdraw altogether from it
Those who are morally conscious with a strong conscience
Those who seek perfection morally, emotionally and spiritually
Many people come to this quest for inner peace but only a few stay on course. Most people drop out for lack of conviction.
Disappointment, disillusionment and disgust with the ways of the world that border on evil is a potent reason for coming to spirituality

UNENDING PLEASURE

Unending pleasure is a utopia, a mirage and not a practical reality. Most people long for it but never get it. Man and machine both suffer wear and tear and decay with time. Even before decay, faults occur from time to time and sufferance results. Nevertheless, hopes never cease and efforts continue to achieve it.

The desire for immortality is a direct result of wanting to have prolonged pleasure. In spite of the fact that we know matter is destructible, we aim to have life's pleasure till eternity. In spiritual parlance, this is sheer ignorance. We also know that all desires for pleasure are not practical and failure to achieve that objective gives rise to anger, frustration and disappointment with life. But still we pursue in our aim to do the impractical. The inherent duality of the system prevents the happening of unending pleasure because it is in the very nature of existence that pleasure must follow pain. Kings and monarchs, with all the power at their command, failed to achieve the goal of unending pleasure. It is only the saints and mystics, with no wealth and no power could do better than the kings because they understood the nature of existence.

Pleasure is of course of three kinds; of body, mind and that of intellect. Pleasure of the body is momentary because the body will tire soon as it needs physical strength. The pleasure of mind can last relatively longer, for one can imagine pleasurable pursuit as long as one desires. Pleasure of intellect is in achievement of intellectual success as that of scientists after discovery or that of philosophers in spreading their view point across people and getting it accepted by them. There is nothing great about physical pleasure as it is a common desire that we share with animals. It is the satisfaction of hunger or mating that one has, which gives the physical pleasure. Every one involved in this knows that it can't last forever. Mental pleasure is an idle pursuit that creates a thought pattern, which may or may not be desirable to the person involved. Those who are in the habit of harming others for self-gain indulge in this kind of sadistic pleasure. Most people indulge in this sometime or the other while some make a habit of this. Only a few turn their thinking to the welfare of others and take pleasure in doing so. These are the ones that change the world for the better. The intellectual pleasure of creation in arts and sciences is the noblest and evolves humanity to new heights. But for this we would have been still living in caves and hunting for food.

All pleasures, whether selfish or ennobling, are temporary, and hence frustrating, because they cannot be continued ad infinitum. Sooner or later they cease and make us frustrated and angry, resulting in disappointment and disillusionment with life as such. That is why seekers of spirituality shun the desire of pleasures, and instead, aim a life in which they treat pleasure and pain on an even keel. The Upanishad states that unfulfilled desire for pleasure generates anger, the anger spoils wisdom and lack of wisdom leads to downfall. The root for downfall therefore lies in the desire for pleasure. That is why Buddha advised all to control desires. Freedom of action and attaining of wisdom is dependent on our ability to master our desires. This is the basis of self-control that enables us to move on and progress on the path of spirituality.

ACTIVITY OF BODY AND MIND

In our worldly life it is important that we work physically to maintain this body in good health. It is also important that we think positively to keep our mind healthy because mind and body are intimately connected. We learn skills to earn money and we spend money to buy food and clothing for the body.

It is our thoughts that drive our actions. It is our intellect that acts a go-nogo circuit to these thoughts, a kind of filter that allows actionable thoughts and stops undesirable ones. Our active life therefore depends on the mind-body-intellect. The extent to which we use our intellect decides our personality. If we acted on all the thoughts that came to mind, we would not be different from animals. The instinctive life is different from intellectual one. As human beings we pride on our intellect, and in a way rightly so.

As we nourish our body and mind with food and intellectual thoughts, we need to nourish our spirit with spiritual practices. The saints and mystics do so by increasing their spiritual activity vis-à-vis physical and mental ones. They take only as much food as is necessary to maintain the body and control their thoughts, ignoring the negative ones and reducing those that involve them with the material world. They have good control over temptations and allurements that take one away from the spiritual path. Spiritual thoughts and prayers that are centered on the Divine amply compensate their physical inactivity. To them all actions are for the service of God.

It is said in Upanishads and Bhagwadgita that those actions that are done selflessly and are offered to God do not generate any Karma. These actions in fact do not qualify for karmic reward whatever their nature is. These are the actions that do not qualify for reward or punishment. The actions of saints and mystics come in this category. The spiritual seeker is advised to stick to such actions alone. In other words, we are advised to shun selfishness and act only in the service of God. This means living in peace and harmony with nature and not disturb the balance of human life with the rest of species, plant or animal. Disturbance of nature's balance is not in the interest of human existence.

Science also confirms that disturbing the balance of nature with our actions is not in the interest of our survival. The last century's progress in technology has done great harm to the ecological balance due to excessive deforestation and over use of the resources of nature. This is in part due to the neglect of spiritual aspect and excessive emphasis on technological development. The role of human existence in nature is over emphasized due to our selfish interest. We no longer care for what happens to others so long as our interests are served. We bully and get what we want. We have developed a consumerist society that prides on consumption. Our economic theories are based on generated needs and not genuine needs. We consume more than required and therefore use up more resources than required. It is a cycle of consumption and production without regard to replenishment.

In the present way of life in the consumerist society, we believe in ceaseless activity of production and consumption. There is no thought on slowing down to reflect and spiritualize. Our desires are overshadowing our genuine needs. In our race to generate more and more wealth we are impoverishing our souls and becoming merely living machines. It is time to adjust the priorities.

SILENCE OF BODY AND MIND

We all know silence is golden when argument turns ugly. It is also desirable when we have nothing to do and indulge in gossip to kill time. Silence saves energy and makes us reflect and think of doing something better. Silence of body implies stilling the movement and silence of mind means stilling thoughts. Silence of body and mind is necessary if we wish to move ahead in spiritual pursuit.

In meditation we use silence of our body and mind. This is basically done to avoid distraction of mind that runs wild in thoughts when body is stilled. The highest state of meditation is when mind becomes thoughtless and our only awareness is of just being. It is of course not easy to bring our body-mind complex in this state. Though various techniques exist to achieve it, every technique requires a great effort in self-control and patience in practice. Not many can achieve success in short time since mind is the most difficult to control. It is particularly more difficult for the extrovert.

Generally it is easier for the introvert to practice silence of the body and mind. It is my experience that you can start with developing a reading habit to exclude the external interference and then slowly get used to remaining silent in a noisy environment. It saves you energy and you become more reflective than reactive. Moving the thoughts to spiritual aspects also helps. Philosophers and thinkers are rarely seen spending time in speech unless forced by circumstances.

Silence of mind is akin to mental death in physical sense but spiritually it is a new life in higher levels of consciousness. This is what mystics tell us. You have to die externally in order to rise internally. The inner world is stated to be more peaceful and more potent in awareness. This is the aim and purpose of spiritual practice. It is an intuitive state of existence in which pure consciousness is the guiding light.

In my personal view, the problems of life will be much reduced if we spoke less and devoted all our actions to God. Speaking less immediately cuts down our quota of speaking ill of others. Meaningless chatter serves no purpose. It is not for nothing that fasting and silence are highly rated in spiritual circles. *Maunvrata,* or vow of silence, is a common spiritual exercise. It enables self-reflection and meditation for spiritual growth. As said earlier, mantras become more potent and more effective when they are recited in silence than loudly. In silence, concentration also increases, giving better results.

Over the years, we have made our life noisier than what it was, say fifty years ago. The traffic noise, the 24x7 TV, the noisier ways of enjoyment and higher wattage of gadgets adds to our problem of noise. Noise pollution now has reached a level that threatens our peaceful existence. People say it is a sign of development but I feel it is symptomatic of reduced spirituality in our life. We have become more restless. Our religion has become more external and showy than silently inward. Technological advancement has gone to our head and we are ignoring our inner being in preference to some material toys. It is time to go inward and reflect.

WILLINGLY ETHICAL

There is an often-cited story about the honesty of people. A king wanted to know how ethical his subjects were. He asked his minister to find out. The minister in turn sent a message to people to donate one glassful of milk for the sake of some worship in the temple. They were to come in the morning with the milk and pour it in a big vessel placed before the deity. In the next morning when the priest came to collect the milk, he found in the vessel nothing but water. Obviously every body thought one glass of water would not be noticed in the milk. The next day the king ordered that every one was to put the milk otherwise there will be punishment to the one who did not comply. The next day the priest was happy to collect the vessel full of milk. Obviously out of fear every one had been honest to the command. The lesson of the story is that people are honest only under pressure and not willingly. Given circumstances to cheat or to deceive they would succumb to the temptation out of personal interest.

Next the king wanted to know how many of his subjects were willingly honest. He ordered that the price of milk could be raised if the milkman feels the need of it. Next day most of the milk vendors had increased the price except a few. These few were the willingly honest. It was obvious that in one day the cost of milk could not rise since production and supply had remained the same.

To be willingly ethical we need to have an inner desire to be so. Most people under fear do things that they would not do otherwise. The desire to be honest, or more generally ethical, arises out of a spiritual bent of mind. Those who live for self and do every action out of selfish interest cannot be willingly ethical. Their personal gain is supreme in all their decisions. Only those that have concern for others can work selflessly.

I do not wish to be sermonizing, but the fact remains that self-interest is generally dominant in the minds of people. Only a few rise above this weakness. The ethical values cannot be forced on people, for fear of authority lasts only temporarily.

To change a society we need to inculcate the values in society through persuasion and example. Ethical values are not only for individual persons but also for communities and nations. If we stuck to some basic ethical values, we could make a noticeable change in the attitude of people and societies.

I am reminded of a friend of mine who once said, 'people are unnecessarily afraid of being honest and straight. They think this way they will lose. But the gain in terms of spiritual benefit is much more than their material loss if any. Problem lies in the fact that we consider spirituality as something foreign to our being. We think it is for some saints and mystics and not for us. We relate it to idealism and not with practical life. We forget that living according to spiritual values is part of our life. These values shape our personality, give it credibility and make us likeable to others. We do not have to put up a show of ethics to people. We only need to be true to ourselves and live a credible life.'

Let us put our share of milk in the cauldron of humanity and be counted among the willingly ethical.

UNWILLING TO BE SPIRITUAL

According to one opinion, the undeveloped minds and unrefined hearts cannot comprehend nor appreciate the philosophy behind spiritual truths. It is partly because they have not had any experience of the intuitive mind. It is useless to put across the spiritual philosophy to them for they lack the equipment to understand or reflect on that.

They have neither the desire nor the inclination to question the meaning and purpose of life. Their mind is incapable of taking flight to the higher aims of life. To counter this incapability to cope with spiritual aims, they resort to offence by criticizing and downplaying the essentials of spirituality as something unreasonable and impracticable. They support their arguments on the basis of science, intellect and sensory experiences. Their criticism at times becomes abusive and downright arrogant. Perhaps it is their Samskaras that prompt them to behave so. They find religious contradictions easy fodder to feed on and confuse spirituality with religion.

In the present age of complexities and competition, lack of time for spiritual issues is a common excuse to avoid the spiritual concerns. Most people hide behind their preoccupation with mundane issues of earning and maintaining theirs and their family's life. They plead lack of time as the excuse to avoid spiritual practice. They even refuse to discuss these issues since they consider them as secondary to their lives. They are the ones who say they have no time to reflect on questions concerning their existence on this planet, why they are here and where they will go after death. They are so absorbed in their duties and responsibilities that they take them to be the be all and end all.

The trivial attractions of the world are increasing by the day because of the advancement of technology. The toys of technology that engage them in entertainment and meaningless information are increasingly occupying their time and energy. Such persons take shelter in their preoccupation with such engagements. In consequence, they spend time without getting anywhere in higher pursuits of life.

The persons who avoid uncomfortable questions of philosophy concerning their life knowingly and deliberately turn to more physical and mental activity to boost their ego and social status. Their ignorance of the spiritual tradition reinforces their dismissive attitude towards spirituality. The fact however is that their consciousness has not expanded enough to make them sensitive to spiritual philosophy. They are unwilling to put any control on their desires, emotions or on the inflated ego.

The discipline required for verifying the claims of mystics is indeed difficult and demands sacrifice of comfort and ease of living. Only a few are willing to go for this. The worldly-minded are skeptical to take up the required training of mind. The lazy ones are not willing to part with their comfortable style of living. The intelligent ones of course are not prepared to wait for the result that is uncertain and distant. They even consider it quite foolish to undergo this journey of self-realization because they never had any spiritual experience to convince them of the vitality of this quest. They ignore the divinity within them and live on the surface to lead a material life.

Those of us who are unwilling to go for spirituality do so because they lack faith in the higher power. For them their material life is the only reality that they recognize. They are not willing to go beyond. Their purpose of life does not include enquiry into the deeper realms of existence. They are happy with their materialism and comfortable life. The very poor and very rich seldom find interest in spirituality because the poor have no time free from earning, and the rich are too busy with their wealth management.

Ideally, one should be able to find some time for higher thoughts after one has achieved a fair degree of material success. Yet the common attitude is to be content with what one has and go no further. People are satisfied if they have the healthy body, enough work, adequate pleasure, a family and some friends and sufficient wealth. Beyond this only a few venture to take their life to questions of higher consciousness, an enquiry about the reality of their existence and a value system to observe sincerely. They find no need for serious thought, study, prayer and meditation. They will go for this only if their health and wealth get affected seriously. The search for truth does not concern them because their thoughts do not go beyond their body, relationships, entertainment and social status.

Surprisingly, those whose escape routs run through cinema, television, radio or theatre consider spirituality as another avenue for escapism. They view spirituality as another commodity for bargain, they will frequently ask, ' what do I get if I become spiritual.'

The enquiry of inner being is a matter of faith and patience. Development of intuitive faculty is not done in a day. Most people, who are not inclined to spirituality, think that it is an abstraction lacking any utility at all. They think that the ideal set for the quest is unreachable. They leave the idea even without trying, for they think the discipline required of them is beyond their mettle. They think in this world of violence, treachery and deceit, it is not practical to live in a divine plane. However, such a view displays only a weakness in mind. Determination can conquer great heights. The unspiritual live only in their sense plane and cannot think beyond material life. Extrasensory life is a puzzle to them, which they are not prepared to solve.

In their cocoon like life, they are not prepared to face the truth and accept it even if it were offered to them by the seers. So long as they remain focused in the physical world, spiritual thoughts will not penetrate their minds.

Generally, persons who belong to the average class of society, neither rich nor poor, those whose mental capacity is nothing to acclaim about, and who suffer at the hands of fate and other sections of society turn to ritual religion rather than religious philosophy. Their affinity for philosophy is almost next to nothing. They have an attraction for rituals and mythology and live on emotions. For such people, spirituality is a means to improve them by self-control. They are afraid to make their own way in the pursuit of spirituality. They feel comfortable in groups and in company of the likeminded. They are the ones who congregate at religious functions in the name of divine dispensation. They follow the tradition, be it religious or social.

For some, spirituality is a direct enemy of their ego. They cannot bear it to attack their desires, passions and infatuations. They are worried that they may have to shed some old habits, which go against the tenets of spirituality. So they take what suits them and discard the rest.

To move on spiritual path, you have to pay the price of self-discipline and shedding of ego. Most people do not want to do this. They are happy being indifferent to spirituality.

WHO ARE YOU?

The chief guest was being introduced to a gathering of people who came to a conference on management. When the guest asked individually, 'who are you' he got the following replies:

'I am the president of the chamber of commerce' said the businessman
'I am the Director of a research laboratory' said the scientist
'I am a servant of God' said the devotee of a temple God
'I am a healer of people' said the doctor
'I am a university professor' said the intellectual
'I am the president of the university students union' said the student
'I am the chief priest of the temple' said the religious head
'I look after all of them' said the hotel manager
'I secure the welfare of people' said the security officer
'I feed people' said the catering manager
'I am trying to find who I am' said the philosopher

There was a person standing aloof in a corner. The guest decided not to ignore any one so he went to him and repeated his question.

'I am all of them. I am the conscious energy present in all living beings. I am the force behind the senses, the consciousness of being.' Said the spiritualist.

THE PLAY OF EGO

THE DESIRE TO OUTSHINE

The world is a playground of ego. The desires are the medium through which ego plays around. The existence as an individual, with a desire to assert one's individuality is itself a play of the ego. Most activities in this world that are done by individuals or groups of individuals are an expression of the ego; be it the learning, working for self or for others or even charity. In childhood the baby cries and asserts its individuality for attention. In school, the student wants to get higher marks for assertion of its talent and superiority over others. The very spirit of competitiveness is a sign of the play of ego. Competition in studies, games and sports and other extracurricular activities are all signs of the play of ego. The sense of pride in achievement, the sadistic pleasure of bullying, the boasting of one's attainments and the desire to dominate are all expressions of the ego playing its game.

In schools of higher learning, the desire to learn skills and its use in later life of earning wealth, the competition with colleagues in the rat race to outwit and outshine others is all dictated by the individual's innate desire to assert one's individuality as a competent worker. The negative traits of using unfair means for rising above others are increased directly in proportion to the boosting of ego. It is therefore understandable if spirituality demands curtailment of ego so as to make life easy for all.

Ego appears where one does not expect it to be present. In charity and other efforts to help the poor and the weak, there lurks the ego in the form of earning acclaim and name as a reward for the good actions. We see eulogizing plaques put on walls, praising the good deeds, or even simply mentioning the name of the donor so as to bring honor to the individual. In fact, in the present world dominated by advertisement, there is hardly any work that does not bring out the ego of the doer. In this advertise or perish situation, people have to advertise their sermons, religious advice and even service to mankind so as to draw attention of others to their good work. Good writing does not get noticed unless it is advertised. Good paintings and good music too need favorable critics to become popular.

It will not be much of an exaggeration to say that ego is behind all work and play in this world. So long as we recognize individuality we accept the role and power of ego. In this age of competitive existence, even saints and mystics are not free of it. Whether alone, or in company, they need wealth and power to stand in status to get noticed.

Is ego really undesirable as the spiritualists say? One has to see it in the proper perspective. So long as you need to exercise your individuality, you cannot get away from the exercise of ego. Spirituality is not about individuality as much as it is for universalism. In spiritual experience one dissolves oneself in the universal existence of Atman, the divine spirit. This act of dissolving will not happen if you keep your individual I-ness intact. You need to completely merge your ego with the collective existence of creation. You do not think for yourself but for all. The well being of all becomes your well being. Your thoughts and your actions all get oriented to the universal life. This is akin to the death of individuality in this world. That is why the spiritualists call shedding of ego as death in the material world and enlightenment as being born to the Divine life.

With the death of individuality dies the sense of individual pride, the competition for material gain and sense of one-upmanship that is so characteristic of ego. It is a matter of choice; you may choose to lead a life of ego and pride and enjoy the transitory enjoyments with inevitable suffering due to the duality of existence or you may opt for the eternal bliss of the spiritually enlightened state of universal existence. The majority however prefers the former since reaching the latter state is difficult, uncertain and time consuming and needs self-discipline of very high order.

THE EGO MIND OF THE INTELLECTUAL

When an intellectual expresses his soul's yearning it comes out in art, culture, poetry, music or scientific discovery. Intellect is the highest point of material mind while intuition is the lowest point of divine mind. A material mind may soar to intellectual heights but the divine mind starts where material mind ends. The divine mind is at once all knowing, full of clarity and intuitive in character. In moving from intellect to divinity, one transits from higher mind to intuitive mind and ego is surrendered to the divine will.

The intuitive flashes of creativity are the expression of the divine consciousness operating in the human mind. Conversely, the human mind too wants to enter the divine consciousness. It is an expression of the development of human mind. Human intellect is at the thin line of separation between the material mind and the divine mind. On one side is the intuitively conscious divine mind while on the other is the materially conscious sense mind. One goes into the divine states through meditation and self-realization.

Body, mind and intellect constitute the material states of existence and in these states ego reigns supreme. Ego of the body state is concerned with the survival of the body and its ornamentation. Food and clothing fulfill this desire. The states of the lower mind are concerned with the emotions of attachment, separation, worldly desires of acquisition, greed, possession and pleasure of the senses. The intellect constitutes the higher states of material mind where thoughts of aspiring to higher states, learning, discernment, pride of achievement etcetera are entertained. Here ego is the uplifting faculty that soars to heights of achievement in different fields of activity. One takes pride in creative writing, scientific discovery, a masterpiece painting, a moving speech, leadership qualities and so on. For the worldly mind this is an asset that takes one to heights of achievement.

But, for the spiritually oriented, even the ego mind of the intellectual is a barrier that needs to be crossed in order to move ahead spiritually. So long as the ego mind persists, the sense of individuality remains strong. When individuality is strong, the feeling of universality will remain dormant and one would remain connected with the pride of the body consciousness. The person would think as an individual, act as individual and universalism will remain only an idea and not a working principle.

The spiritually conscious will think universal and act universal. To him the welfare of others will be as much relevant as the welfare of the individual self.

To most persons living in material consciousness, intellect is the high point of existence. But for the spiritual aspirant, one has to rise above this level and go over to the intuitive state of spiritual consciousness. There are still higher levels of universal consciousness and God consciousness that have to be reached. The highest point of course is to scale the peak of Divine truth and live in pure consciousness. Thus while the material mind is satisfied with the high point of intellect with its ego association, the spiritually oriented starts from this point and moves ahead into the intuitive levels to reach the spiritually high point of pure consciousness.

THE PHILOSOPHER

He was a learned man. He had a degree from a foreign land, and had published a number of papers in religious philosophy. His fame extended beyond the boundary of his native land. He was author to many books. People respected him for his knowledge and scholarship. In his field of study and research he was considered an authority. People sought him for conferences and literary discussions and honored him to earn a name for them. He was an intellectual by any standard of reckoning. His students were spread far and wide. I too had a respect for him, not only for his academic brilliance but also for his human qualities as well. Considering his age and his professorial status, I called him the guru.

I often had discussions with him on spiritual aspects because he had read the scripture of his religion in minute detail. Not only his religion, he could talk authoritatively on other religions too. He had made a comparative study of the world's most known religions and could enlighten me on many aspects of their good points. I enjoyed his company, for he was quite objective in his inferences and logical in his elaborations.

One day I was having my evening walk along the Palm Avenue. It was so named because it had palm trees lined along both sides of the avenue. Most persons of my age and my temperament preferred this place for a walk. It was silent, clean and salubrious. I had hardly gone about half the distance of my usual length of walk when I saw him strolling with a friend. I greeted him with reverence and he smiled back. He was talking to his friend on the need to cultivate the habit of rational thinking on both scientific and religious matters even though religion survived on faith. His argument was that in this age of science and logic, religion needed to be interpreted through rational thought since people had become used to the ways of science and technology. His friend of course did not agree to that. His friend said that changing times do not change religion as it is founded on prophetic sayings. According to him conservatism is an inseparable part of religious thinking. I felt that this discussion was going in the well-grooved pattern of thought and needed a change of direction. I therefore said,

'What do you think, Professor, is the relationship of spirituality and learning. Does learning improve the chances of spiritual experience?'

The professor turned his face towards me and said,' the answer is both yes and no. It is yes if you want to be enlightened about the essentials of religion, the reality of existence and the knowledge about the need of spirituality in one's life. But the answer is no if you are going for pure experience of the spiritual state of enlightenment, the state of self realization or the Nirvana as the Buddhists call it or the state of Samadhi as the yogis call it. The reason is that it is very difficult to get over the ego attached to the state of learning. How many learned people can claim to be free of ego-linked thoughts about their knowledge and learning. Moreover, even an illiterate person can have spiritual experience. What is required is the state of universal love and compassion for the whole humanity, which has nothing to do with one's learning or scholarship. Upanishads tell us that one can rise to the divine state of enlightenment by purely devotional practice to the one and only reality of our existence. This path of devotion bypasses the intellectual learning as many religious philosophers have pointed out. Even in the knowledge path one needs to leave the intellect and go over to the intuitive mode to progress further in the spiritual journey. The intellectual path has a high probability of ego obstructing the path of spiritual progress. It is human failing to feel proud of one's achievement. Pride of learning and knowledge can therefore prevent one's progress towards spiritual advancement.'

'But is not the knowledge path one of the three paths to salvation? This is a path that comes naturally to an intellectual. Why must then it be abandoned for fear of the associated ego?' I said this to clarify the point.

'Yes, it is true that *gyan marg* is a recognized path of spirituality and especially suited to the enquiring mind. But it must be followed with utmost humility and knowledge must be perceived as a gift of God. There must not be any trace of pride or feeling of superiority about it. Intelligence must be seen as something obtained by the grace of God and not as an advantage gained by one's achievement. It is very difficult to suppress the pride born out of one's learning. Many a learned persons have fallen a prey to this weakness of human mind.'

It was indeed interesting to see that he knew the danger of ego boosting in his achievements.

After hearing him, I felt more convinced about his greatness. Being an intellectual of great merit, he also knew the pitfalls of great learning and fame. I wished the two friends all the best and came back thinking of the various ways ego hides in ones achievements.

THE LAWYER PRIEST

It was a coal tar road, straight and long, running through the desert country. I was traveling in a car on government business. The heat and sand was oppressive. The tar was beginning to melt with the heat of the desert. Whatever water I had brought was finished and I needed to refill on emergency basis. I asked the driver, who was well aware of the local conditions, where to find water. He replied that there were a few huts some two km away and there was a small temple there where we could rest and refill our water bottle. He said he knew the priest there and we will not face any problem. I asked him to try that option even if it meant spending more time on the journey.

When we reached the place, we were greeted by the priest. He obviously knew that we had come to get either water or pay our respect to the deity or may be both. After resting a while and filling our water bottle, I asked him how he managed to live under such severe conditions. It was more of a ruin than a habitable building. The water was scarce and heat was oppressive. There did not seem to be a source for daily food either. Except for a few huts some distance away and a roof overhead there was no sign of civilized life anywhere. It was nothing but an invitation to discomfort and uncertain living. Sensing my feelings about the place the priest smiled and said,' you must be thinking why I chose this place for settling down. But if I had not done so, how would you be having your water and rest at this place. Actually, it is not so bad. Every day I get one or two devotees who bring something to eat and offer their prayers to the deity. It is a peaceful life, though a little uncertain of food supply, but it is alright with me since I can live without eating for a day or two.'

From the appearance of the priest it looked as if he was educated and had lived in cities for some time. His manner of speaking and the language used showed his good upbringing. I therefore felt inquisitive about his background. Risking a rebuff, I asked him what brought him to that place. This made him pensive for some time and finally he asked, ' are you really interested in my personal life? Perhaps, you know that it is not wise to ask a holy man his past since in most cases it is tragic and not worth reviving the emotions.' I apologized to him for touching his raw nerve but I was really curious how a well brought up man landed in this environment. I therefore said that it was indeed up to him to answer me or not.

Slowly he came round to normality and said, ' I shall make an exception and tell you my background since you are so keen to know. Back in the city some hundred kilometers away from this place, I was a criminal lawyer having a flourishing practice in the district court. I was quite well off and famous in the adjoining districts for my ability to let people get off from harsh sentences. I have no hesitation to say that I saved many criminals from punishment by manipulating law, as was my profession. People in the business of cheating and murder admired my skills to get them off the hook. I amassed plenty of money, though ill gotten in the eyes of others. But it was work and I enjoyed doing it. The life was moving smoothly and I was proud to be a person of status in the society, which treated me well. But as you know, pleasure is often followed by pain and I was no exception to that. Two years back our only child, a son, expired in an accident that left us shattered. As if it was not enough, a year later my wife also passed away leaving me all alone to mourn and suffer the pangs of loneliness. I therefore decided to leave that place and started on a journey to another city. It was only on this road, just like you, that I happened to meet a person who advised me to take a rest and freshen up in this temple. I followed his advice and met the then priest who put me on the path of spirituality, which changed the course of my life. Seeing the simple, and high thinking, life of that priest impressed me a lot. I then decided to stay here as an assistant to that priest. I found over a time that my pride in my ability as a lawyer was indeed misplaced. There are things beyond one's control and sooner or later one is driven to a state when he needs the help of a superior power. This life at the temple gave me a peace of mind that I had lacked in my earlier life. I learnt a lot from my senior colleague about the reality of life. I am happy that I took the decision to stay here. I realized that a man does not live by bread alone. There are things that make a man wiser about the true meaning of life. The surprising thing about the life here is that the loneliness here is not a pain but is a pleasure. The books on spirituality left by my senior priest give me company that I cherish a lot. Perhaps, in your position you cannot appreciate what I am saying, but I speak from my heart and what I say is the truth. Silence, contentment and study of books give me company. I am now at peace with my soul. I can only wish you a safe journey and happiness in your life'

Hearing him gave me an experience that I value even now. Indeed there are values in life that are sometimes not shared nor appreciated. There is no better experience than finding peace within.

INTELLECT AND SPIRITUALITY

'In the material world intellect plays an important part. The person with intellect has a better chance of success than the one without it. But in spirituality, intellect has no significant advantage. Why?'

'It is because intellect interacts with material environment, with material objects and living beings. Spirituality deals with inner being. In meditative state or the samadhi, one is in the state of thoughtlessness and has object free awareness. Intellect has no relationship with this state. But to the seeker, intellect plays a part in the preliminary studies and discernment of what is true and what is false. The one with intellect can study the scriptures and know the value of spiritual pursuit. Beyond this it gives no advantage. In fact to reach higher consciousness, one has to leave the ladder of intellect and go for thoughtless meditation'.

'What is the difference between a spiritual person and an unspiritual one? Does ego affect both equally?'

'The spiritual person believes that the true nature of man or woman is the spirit and not the body, mind or intellect. The unspiritual person disagrees with it and thinks that our reality is the body-mind-intellect. The spiritual one has strong belief in the universal values of existence, like truthfulness, universal love and concern for others etcetera. The unspiritual one may or may not believe in these values.'

'Do rationality and spirituality mix together?'

'Some people think that to be unspiritual is to be rational and scientific minded or vice versa. But this is an erroneous impression created by writings that equate logic and reason with scientific thinking and faith and religion with lack of reason. However, religion and spirituality is not the same thing. Spirituality is essentially connected with inner reality and it has nothing to do with outward show of religiosity such as rites and rituals. A rational mind may also be spiritual. To equate rationality with denial of faith is a misconception, which is often found among people who have only surface knowledge of spirituality, religion and faith.'

'Why does a scientist generally deny the faith and labels himself as rational?'

'To be rational is not the same thing as faithless. One may adopt a faith after getting convinced of the truth. An enlightened person can have faith in the supreme power through experiencing it, even though he may not be able to define it nor correctly describe it. A scientist on the other hand, may not experience the spiritual truth and deny its existence even without taking the trouble of going through spiritual practices. The experience of divinity may require years of spiritual training, which a scientist may refuse to undergo. Such a person has no reason to call the spiritual person as illogical or whimsical. Without trying the spiritual path it is unfair to deny the spirit its existence within. The inward looking person has his own way of experiencing it that is real to him.'

'Do ethics and morality have importance for the spiritual person alone?'

'No. They are relevant to all, spiritual or otherwise. But for spiritual person they have special significance because without ethics and morality in place one cannot start the spiritual practices. If done so, they may harm the person spiritually and obstruct his progress on the path to self-realization.'

'According to the sages every one is destined to reach the goal of spirituality, though it may take different time for different people. If it is so, then why worry about spiritual practices and the personal discipline?'

'It is true that as part of evolution, all living beings are destined to evolve to the highest state of consciousness. But the time required varies with the state of being. For those who are at the lowest ladder of consciousness it may take many births or even centuries to evolve to the highest state. For those who have already covered some ground by practicing spirituality, the required time may be considerably less. For some highly evolved beings, they may even rise to the highest state in this life itself. To reach a high state, the practice of spirituality is necessary. This includes self improvement by way of achieving high level of personal and social conduct, meditative practices to experience spiritual growth and so on.'

'Is self realization same as becoming one with God?'

'Self-realization means knowing and experiencing the true nature of oneself that is the spirit and not the body. This spirit is universal and the ultimate reality of every being. At this level of knowledge, one is truly universal and not the egoistic individual. This in a way is becoming one with the reality that is the universal consciousness. One could call this reality God or pure consciousness depending upon one's concept of God. Becoming one with that reality, is like merging with this reality, and losing one's individual status as a material being.'

WHO IS DEARER TO GOD?

It was an old temple that had a spacious compound, a big pond, an idol of stone and a deep sanctorum. It had an equally old priest who religiously performed the duties to the temple and to the lord. There were fixed hours for opening and closing the temple and the visitors and devotees could not directly enter the sanctorum. There were small cubicles all around the sanctorum for those who wanted to silently meditate on God. There was also a big hall where religious ceremonies were performed. People gathered for God's blessings both in the evening and in the morning. The evening prayers were, however, special as a number of lamps were lit that produced a very pleasing sight. The specialty of this temple was that it gave shelter to those who had nowhere to go and who depended on the mercy of others for their survival.

A trust managed the temple and by the grace of God there was no shortage of funds.

Among those dependent on the temple was a person who stayed in one of the cubicles but did not partake in any of the temple ceremonies or the daily *puja* services. He remained in his cubicle and meditated whenever he liked. The rest of the time he just wandered, as he liked. The visitors and devotees thought him to be a beggar spending his days on the income of the temple. However, he did some odd jobs for the priest to justify his food that he took from the temple funds.

One day the priest called him and said, 'I have to go to my village on an emergency. Could you kindly take on my responsibilities for a week? Whatever people may think of you, I am of the opinion that you are the best person to serve the God because you are a person of good conduct and spend all your time in reflection and meditation on God. I know that most of the visitors, and daily devotees, who come here, only make a show of their devotion and forget God as soon as they go back to their work. I need a person who is clean and clear at heart to do this duty since it is a sacred work.' The beggar looking man agreed to do the work in the spirit of a servant of God but said he will not be as ritualistic as the priest had been. He assured him however, that he would do his best.

Two days passed without any incident. But on the third day, a trustee attended the evening prayers. He asked the people why the priest was not there and who was this beggar looking person that substituted for the priest. People told him that the man was staying at the temple but looks to be an atheist since he never attended any religious ceremony when the priest was there. This enraged the trustee and he ordered that this man should not be allowed to perform the pujas.

A frail looking man was witnessing all this commotion. When he saw that the poor man was being divested of his duties, he said, ' how can you say that this man is an atheist. I have seen him meditating for most of the day whereas most other people hardly remember God for more than fifteen minutes a day. Moreover, I would like to know who is dearer to God? This man here who devotes most of his time in meditation or the priest who does *puja* for half an hour in the morning and half hour in the evening. In my opinion there is no better person than this man to do the *puja*. Moreover, the priest himself appointed him for this job because he knew that this man is the fittest person for the job. It is not necessary to show your love of God outwardly to earn His praise. If you know He is always within you, there is no better way than to meditate on Him. This could be done in silence and loneliness. To worship the idol, it is not necessary to stand before it. You can visualize it in your mind and say the prayers.'

I think what the frail looking man said was justified in view of the omnipresent nature of God. But the ritually oriented persons failed to see the point. This is how the religion is practiced. Even today I am not sure who is dearer to God, the priest or the meditator? If you know, then do tell me.

NON-CONFIRMISM IN SPIRITUALITY

In the world of egoists, it is known that spiritual seekers are in minority because they seek the difficult task of self-realization that requires diminishing of ego. This causes nonconformity in the behavior of the seeker vis-à-vis the majority way of life. It therefore requires a certain amount of courage on the part of the seeker to move ahead in his path of spirituality. Even otherwise, the path of spiritual seeker is unworldly in the sense that it is oriented towards universality while the majority follows the individualistic path of materialism.

The seeker must fulfill his social obligations without breaking the social conventions. He must find a solution to the problem of living in society without becoming a slave to its traditions and conventions. The defiance of society must be in a persuasive and positive sense and not the confrontationist negative sense. It is but natural that he must move away from such conventions that take him towards materialism. A passive attitude to materialistic ideas will do the trick. There is no need to break conventions in dress or body language. The change is needed in thoughts and not in outward show. He must adopt simplicity as the basis of living. Pompous and costly living is to be avoided. His individuality must be reflected in the simple living and high thinking, a thinking of spiritual ideas, and study of spiritual thought.

The physical activity may be replaced by reflection and meditation. Blind imitation of others views can be avoided and one's discerning mind can be exercised for deciding what is right and what is wrong. He must weigh his upbringing in materialistic society against the new path that is entirely spiritual. He must not waver against the pressures of society that propel him to a materialistic life. His conviction should stand him in good stead. His standing alone in the crowd of materialists is an indication of his resolve to pursue his path with sincerity and determination. It is indeed difficult to counter the materialist *samskaras,* but to succeed in the mission it is necessary to take drastic steps towards the progress to spiritual goal.

With time, the seeker stands out more lonely and private than the materialistic crowd around him. The materialistic suggestions and opinions of others around him have to be fought against the better judgment of the seeker. The seeker has to develop his intelligence against the overpowering suggestions to the contrary. He has to seek his path against temptations and persuasions of his materialist friends Conventional religious and social traditions are often strong factors pinning the seeker down. Such obstructions need to be tackled with tact and determination, even to the arrogance of the close ones.

The seeker's inner life is not shared by any one. He is to be guided by his conviction and his priorities. The greatest problem comes in shedding the ego that rules the materialist world. One must freely choose one's path against heavy odds of society, family and friends. It is futile to seek guidance from those who are reluctant to move on the path of spirituality. One must not be shy of changing gurus or the religious beliefs from one to another if the inner reality beckons to do so. Any hesitation or doubt is not good for the pursuit of the spiritual goal. Only the clear heart and a clean mind can take one further to his goal of achievement.

The institutional goals of a religion may not agree with the quest of the individual seeker. It is an individual effort and one's inner convictions play an important part in achieving success. Self-analysis and self-effort are of prime importance. The prevailing ideas about a certain path or a certain direction may not be suited to the differently able individual, who is different in physical abilities and mental training than the rest.

THE SEEKER'S PRAYER AND HOPE

Please do not hide from me
For I know you are there
Hiding behind five sheaths
Guiding me, making me alive

People tell me I can reach you
Rising above body, mind and intellect
Going up in intuition, realizing your truth
Through perseverance, meditation and faith

I seek your grace to succeed
I seek your blessing to proceed
I close my eyes and block my ears
To see your light and hear your voice

Do not disappoint me
For I long your sight
Do not disappoint me
For I know you are kind

I am limited by the senses
But you are infinite and true
I wait with baited breath
Take me with you or show me your light

INNER BEING AS THE SPIRITUAL GURU

The train was moving fast. Most of the passengers in my coach were dozing. It was a rocky terrain and nothing green was visible on both sides of the track. I too was about to doze off when the occupant of the seat next to me suddenly asked a strange question. He said,' do you have a spiritual guru?' I said I did not have one but very much wanted to have one if I could get a good person that fulfilled my idea of a good guru. This encouraged him to say, 'be sure to adopt only the right one since I have recently been duped by such a person. I believed in him and he took advantage of me.' I sympathized with him and said,' it is always difficult to find a good guru who shows us the direction in our spiritual pursuit and helps us at every difficult step. People generally look to saints and mystics as their guru to seek protection and favor in their material life, hardly realizing that the guru is to teach us the spiritual lesson and take us forward in our spiritual journey. People please them to seek boons, favors in business expansion, have blessings for their dear ones and so on. Having got a guru, they forget their spiritual responsibilities and never try to sincerely follow their advice for spiritual awareness. When it comes to meditation and improvement of self conduct, they become careless, for they know that their guru will protect them from bad times.'

'If that is so, is it not desirable to forget a human being as the guru and go for one's conscience as the guru.' He said.

'Yes, I think you have a point.' I said and continued, ' those who are without a guru but are genuinely interested in spirituality find themselves at times rudderless in their pursuit. Even when they want to have a guru, their intellect comes in the way to judge the credentials of the person claiming to be a guru. Their personal ego may prevent them to become a disciple of another person unless they are sure about the spiritual level of the person. For such a seeker, it is suggested that he take his conscience as the guide and move further in his spiritual pursuit without waiting for the right person. Some persons may equate the conscience with the inner being or the Atman that serves the purpose of the guide. In fact, there have been many cases where people have become enlightened by solely relying on their own discrimination faculty and conscience as the guide. After all, the first mystic must have relied only on his faculties to reach the goal. As one progresses on the path, his inner vision becomes sharper and his conscience becomes louder to guide him in his path. This intuitive faculty is indeed the best friend and guide for those who find it hard to get a real master to take them along the path of self-realization. It is also known that guru only shows the direction, the journey has to be traveled by the seeker himself. No success is obtained without personal effort, least of all the difficult one like the spiritual awakening.'

'I agree, the onus of success lies equally, if not more, on the seeker himself. The individual's reflection and self-analysis plays an important part in spiritual attainment. His self-confidence and faith in inner reality go a long way in moving to the desired goal.'

'The spiritual seeker must know that he is not for reforming the world but for reforming himself. The seeker of truth is like a scientist; he tests by experiment. In the case of the spiritual seeker, the experiment is on self and not on external objects.

Spiritual seeking is an individual quest. One finds the reality by oneself, alone in the privacy of his heart, not in public association. Customs, traditions, conventions and habits enslave mankind. One must listen to his conscience and act.

A true seeker charts his course uninfluenced by dogma or sectarian advice. A seeker must ensure that his independent intellectual study, a refusal to be committed to known ways and maintenance of an open mind does not go overboard and lead to spiritual pride that causes obstruction in his path. When others present many paths, listen to the conscience; no matter how great are the authorities one ignores.

For someone without a teacher or guru, the God within acts as the guide. For the independent seeker, or the individual with no master, the inner light is the guide at every step. It is even said that a person need not accept any human leadership if he listens to his inner voice. The inner voice becomes audible to him only if he clears his head and heart and meditates.

Merely following a guru outwardly, without going inward, one cannot get much ahead spiritually. One must know that guidance comes from higher consciousness and not from another human. Guru is also in tune with higher consciousness when he guides. Books, masters and religious ceremonies are only external inputs. For enlightenment, what counts is the inner vision. Without it the goal is not reached. What one cannot get from religion one must get from deeper self through mysticism. In truth, there is only one master and that is the Divine self.'

We would have continued our talk but soon the train slowed down for the next station. It happened to be the destination of my co-passenger. I therefore bade good-bye to him and dozed off.

AVENUES OF TRUTH

DIFFERENT PATHS

Just as there are a number of opinions about a social issue and a number of theories about a physical event, there are many alternative paths to the practice of spirituality. There are individual teachers belonging to different sects and creeds, different religious beliefs, different traditions and different institutions founded to preach a specific belief system, different schools of thought about the aim of life, different ways to practice a certain belief, so on and so forth. In all this jungle of opinions, sects, beliefs and institutions, one needs to find a specific way to move on to achieve the desired goal. Generally, a person of intellect will study the different options and will chart out his own path to follow. There are of course many who get carried away by a particular stream or a particular teacher to start the journey without making a proper assessment of options.

Becoming a slave to one opinion or one school of thought without assessing others, will severely limit the person in knowledge and achievement. It is also possible that a given system or the path that one religiously follows may end in greater confusion that the one with which one started. Also, one may come across a dishonest, or ignorant or even half-baked teacher who may put the seeker astray. Choosing the correct path is therefore a serious issue and a good amount of effort needs to be put in to study, experience and accept the desired way. The same applies to choosing a guru. There are some definite requirements that need to be fulfilled before one becomes a spiritual teacher. Like any teaching assignment, it is a responsible job to lead students to the right direction of achievement. Many a false gurus have caused frustration among the serious students of yoga and spirituality. One needs to carefully study and choose the desired philosophy and practice of spirituality.

Religious fanaticism arises from the belief that there is only one truth, one religion, one prophet or one source of truth, and one way of life that is correct and all others are wrong. This is a typical way of closing the mind, closing all channels of fresh thought and breathing the stale air of a closed room.

A fanatic denounces the fact of history, other thoughts, other opinions and any fresh air from other directions as foul. He is a one track of mind that refuses the help of others in the belief that they will deviate him from his way of thinking. He firmly believes that there is only one path to truth and that path is the one that he is traveling on. He is a man with self-imposed blinkers. His eyes and ears are closed to others' experiences. In matters of religion he believes that what other religions and sects know, and practice, is false. To him other teachings, books, or mystical experiences are a pack of lies. He is unaware of the fact that truth is infinite; it can have infinite aspects and that other practitioners of faith in diverse streams can also have their truth that is as real as his own.

He does not know that inspirations can come in many forms, dispersed in space and time. Truth can be present at different times in different geographical situations. Different lands and different cultures can contribute to human experiences that are different in their own way but true all the same in their own environment. Different prophets, different teachers, different saints can give the truth that is applicable to different people. It is meaningless to stand on one pedestal and be arrogant about one's stand. A wise person appreciates diverse opinion and assimilates the different views for one's advantage. Light is light when it comes from an electric bulb, a flame or a candle or even from the sun. One must appreciate the warmth and brightness instead of criticizing the source.

A true seeker must tap every source of knowledge, every book, every teacher, every saint and every prophet. Pearls can be collected from different seas and still they will remain pearls. The variety adds to the wealth of knowledge and experience of the collector. Sticking to one source of inspiration alone may limit the scope of expansion. It is not for nothing that nature provides variety. One must learn from nature to expand the variety of thought and experience and rise in consciousness. Even though there may be vested interests, the variety of thought exposes the weakness of untruth and enriches the aspirant with higher truth. One must keep one's intellectual liberty intact.

One can learn the basic truths of other systems without actually joining them. You may learn from other cultures and sects without becoming part of their sectarian attitudes. It is advisable to exercise one's discerning power in filtering truth from untruth in various thought streams. Without joining institutional set ups, you may learn the truth they propagate, enrich the store of knowledge and be enlightened of the truth. Keeping your freedom of choice, you may sift and adopt the values, know the common thread running into different thoughts, and gain by this experience.

INDEPENDENCE IN CHOICE OF PATH

Among the many avenues leading to the truth, one must study with an open mind and chart out an independent path that suits the psyche of the person. Vedantic thought supports freedom of the individual to choose the path that one likes to pursue. The object of attention is limitless and timeless. It cannot be confined to the limits of sects or institutions. It is a search for truth through the philosophic path. It is not a religion in the sense of conventionality or orthodoxy.

Binding to any group or sect burdens a person. He must seek independence of approach, broaden his thought and widen his spiritual experience to move on the path suited to his mental and physical make up. It must also be relevant to his spiritual belief. Let every one find his own God, a God that is part of him, a God that shares his life and thoughts, and lives with him every moment of his life.

The path to spiritual awakening is individual, essentially lonely and confined to inner self. Religion only helps to show the way. Groups, organizations, sects, cults, creeds, societies and institutions provide a variety of the views, advices, experiences and directions of movement. But the individual has to make a choice and move on his chosen path.

Most of the major religions of the world believe in the one- God principle, though some have multigod worship as an expression of their religious belief.

The real idea behind multigod worship is that one can choose the right form of God's image for concentration of thought. Every one has a different liking of form. One can choose whatever one likes best and then concentrate his thought on that form to elevate his consciousness. Multiplicity is only for making a choice. There is no point in worshiping all forms at the same time since it would diffuse the thought process and interfere with the concentration. Having chosen a specific form, one must worship the same form or meditate on the same form for better results. Philosophically speaking, the chosen form is not the right presentation of God's imagery or a correct way of representing God. It is only a symbolic way of limiting the limitless and giving a shape to the infinite and eternal for mental visualization that helps to concentrate thought.

One God principle finds its expression in understanding God. Some believe Him as an almighty figure sitting in heaven and dispensing justice to the mortals for their actions. Others consider Him to be an omnipresent force that is conscious of people's affairs and answering to their prayers and pleadings. Still others know Him to be the light, limitless in scope that runs the universe according to certain laws that are inviolable. Somewhat similar to this concept is the scientific view of primordial energy that manifests in material beings as the ultimate reality of this universe. The essential difference between scientific reality and God of religion is the consciousness attached to the God principle. The God principle is seen in the light of human consciousness as a kind of supreme being responsible for material existence while in the scientific view it is an energy field that is present every where.

Coming back to the choice of path, among all the sects, groups, institutions and sectarian organizations, one must remain independent and hold a view, unprejudiced and uncompromised. Other views can be studied for broadening one's view but total attachment with one view will compromise the independence of thought. One should be an enquirer and not a follower of a specific cult. Such labeling, limits and binds the individual to the whims and fancies of the cult. It also prejudices one against other religions and creeds. Cults, creeds, religions, sects and societies present a bewildering and confusing picture of reality. One must therefore, exercise one's own judgment and not be a blind follower of any one.

The inner content of any philosophy must be felt intuitively and grabbed intellectually. A philosopher (literally a lover of wisdom) makes his own path and does not become a meek follower of a trodden path.

Finding one's own path should not lead to over confidence in one's capability. The element of humility should never be lost since ego is the main hurdle in spiritual pursuit. Intellect and self-confidence should never lead to pride, arrogance or irreverence to the masters. . Some one has rightly said that the independence of mind has its own problems; it may lead to stubbornness in error, arrogance in behavior and fanaticism in attitude. Over dependence on intellect and personal strength should never overshadow the help of higher power.

For a person to pursue the independent path, one needs to be wise, balanced, judicious and discriminatory. Wisdom requires higher knowledge, intuitional feeling and intellect. The person following the independent path needs courage to face the criticism of others and to stand up to the power of the established organizations. This fearless courage is possible only if the seeker does not expect any favor from others. Self-reliance and dependence on higher power may look paradoxical but both are needed to move ahead in spirituality. In following an independent path, the seeker may have to wade through mistaken teachings, ambitious teachers, and keep one's intellectual integrity and spiritual independence intact.

INNER BEING AS THE TEACHER

Many people desirous of seeking inner reality have asked this question 'should they be a hermit or remain a householder in their pursuit of spirituality'. The answer to this is not straightforward. It depends on the intellect, level of knowledge and understanding and the ethical standard of the person concerned. May be if you are totally ignorant about spirituality and what it means to you, you may seek the advice of a spiritual guru and go by his advice. But if you are well informed, have a good intellect, have studied the spiritual literature, have indulged in meditation, daily prayers and live a simple life with ethical standards, you can move along the spiritual path remaining a householder and yet be spiritually aware. But if you are at the cross roads and you do not know where to turn next, you can seek guidance from a renowned teacher. One must remember however, that over reliance on a teacher and lack of self-confidence is not going to help one either.

One can aspire for, and achieve enlightenment, by remaining in the house or in ashram. Both a layman and a hermit have equal possibility of being spiritually awakened. It is the heart and mind that should seek spirituality. As for deciding whether to remain a householder and seek spiritual path or be a hermit to do the same, depends on the inner voice that guides you in such matters. External renunciation of the monk style is only expediency rather than an absolute principle of spirituality. The purification of mind can be accomplished at home or in ashram. Renunciation should originate from inner feeling and not from outward appearance. A life of simplicity, humility and celibacy with detachment at heart can be tried at home too. One can fulfill the responsibilities to the family and parents without neglecting the spiritual goal. Householders have an equal right and capacity to lead a holy life. It is not the sole preserve of the monks.

A teacher or the guru is for guidance but the path has to be traversed by the seeker himself. Reliance on self is as important as that on the enlightened ones. The guidance must come either from the conscience or from the enlightened. Prayer, meditation, study and right living will earn the grace of God. Add to this the intuitive guidance and the seeker will sail through. Nature helps us to evolve spiritually slowly but surely. We must however have faith in the Divine that has an invisible hand behind every move.

THE INSTITUTE

In the summer months I had gone to a holy city on the bank of the river Ganges. It was to seek solace from the humdrum of life. One evening when I was taking a stroll on the bank of the river, I noticed a big sign on a wooden board that said' institute of yoga and spirituality. I felt curious about the place because I am inclined to know what these institutions really teach. As I moved near the place, a hefty person of good build who questioned my motive of coming to the institute interrupted me. I told him I was keen to meet the head of the institution since I am interested in the subject of spirituality. He suggested that I should first get an appointment from the Principle's office. I did as he suggested and got an appointment for the next day in the morning.

Next day I got up early and had my bath in the river and got ready to meet the head of the institute of spirituality. At the appointed hour I presented my self to the Principle and told him I was interested to know what was taught at the university. He told me that the institute offered courses of different durations in yoga and spirituality and asked me to take the information from the office. However, I was more inclined to know the philosophy of teaching and not in the details of the courses. So I asked him,' do you take students to lead them to self-realization, for that is the aim of spirituality? If so it is a tall order for this may take an uncertain time for maturity and not many may succeed in the finite time of the courses.' He said yes but the courses were only in the nature of introduction to spirituality and were not meant to turn out accomplished sages.

I must admit that his answer did not satisfy me. I therefore decided to take a detailed look into the syllabi of the courses. I went to their office and collected the brochure. When I read it I was rather amused to find great claims made on spiritualization of the entrants and the high fees charged against that. To me it looked like any private institution that worked more like a business proposition than an academic one. Again, the nature of courses under the title of spirituality was such that I wondered if they could count as spiritual efforts. Topics related to astrology, well being, yoga practices for the health conscious were clubbed in the training of spirituality which had hardly any concern to the practice of spirituality. There was very little emphasis on the deeper aspects of meditation or on self-realization. In fact there was more to do with external work than inward looking practices. I was rather disappointed to see such cursory treatment meted out to so important a subject as self-improvement through spiritualization. When I enquired about the faculty to teach the subjects, I could not find a single name of reputed spiritualist. When I enquired about the success of the institution I was told that it was doing great business since in the present age more and more people were getting interested in spirituality to seek peace of mind. I then realized that selling peace of mind had indeed become a great business and both foreign and Indians persons were falling for it. It pained me to see how commercialism had taken over the noble aims of our sages and saints.

Spirituality was meant for the high minded to uplift them in consciousness through personal discipline to a state of divine consciousness. Here it was a commodity for sale and that too at a high price for a very low aim of stress reduction. The craze for monetary gains can really bring down lofty ideals to mundane level. There was no teaching of the Upanishads and no philosophical content about spirit within us. The subjects that were offered in the name of spirituality amazed me. All the hard work of deep meditation was taken out and substituted with some postures of yoga and some talk about good conduct and relaxation. This is like selling brass in the name of gold.

This is not a lone incident that I have narrated. There is a general tendency among people to downgrade spirituality to the level of another means of stress reduction. The high ideal of self-realization is over looked because it requires a high degree of self-control and deep meditation over long periods. The opportunists and modern marketers have embarked on the idea of making it a commodity for sale to the over stressed individuals in the corporate culture. . The high aim of expansion of consciousness is ignored in preference to the more mundane desire of having mental peace. Let the leaders of religion and teachers of spirituality think over this change in perception and apply the course correction.

THE NEED TO CHANGE

We were walking on the beach casually sipping the coconut water and wondering about the vast expanse of sea that extended right up to the horizon. Suddenly my friend asked me,' do you know that science does not believe in conscious force behind all this magnificence of nature and says it is all an accident. I wonder how all this vast and beautiful nature could come up without any conscious force. People call it God, but I think whatever name you give it, it is a marvelous feat of nature that it is all going like a clockwork with all the different species existing in this world, all the heavenly bodies moving according to fixed laws of nature and the existence of matter in space and time extending beyond our imagination. Even the mathematical formulation of nature by the scientists is beyond the capacity of ordinary person to comprehend.'

I could see my friend turning philosophical, because in moments such as these, it is but natural to wonder at the magnificence of nature, its vastness, its regularity and orderliness, its mystery and complexity that baffles even the best of minds. I therefore joined him in this mood and said, 'it is not the first time that people have wondered at nature. From times immemorial, people have tried to know the force behind nature; the consciousness in the living matter, the evolution, the decay, and the cyclic nature of events and phenomena and the mysterious paranormal happenings beyond the understanding of the human mind. Science has unraveled a lot and promises to do more, but still there are areas that have remained unexplored and unexplained. People still believe in a superhuman force they call as God. In every epoch and every century there have been saints and mystics who have delved into the mystery called God and devised techniques to reach and understand Him. They have exhorted people to follow certain disciplines and experience God through meditation. People even institutionalized these disciplines and established religions. All these efforts were made to understand and experience the mystery of universal consciousness and the complex forces that work behind creation of material world. Any number of paths was devised to reach that mysterious entity called God. Many seekers of truth tried and a few succeeded. The religious beliefs spread and continued. Even today a number of persons are concerned with the spiritual aspect of life and are curious to know what lies behind our existence. They form hypotheses and experiment with spiritual practices to know the truth. This quest for truth has lasted centuries of human evolution and people still pose important questions that need answers. The history of self-realization is long and continuous. There are still believers and nonbelievers of the answers given by sages of yesteryears.'

'I know that religion has had a long tradition of belief and enquiry. But what is the aim of this self-enquiry? I asked.

My friend was quick to respond, 'the ultimate aim is to be led by Atman, the inner divine nature of man, and not by his ego. The fundamental task is to improve oneself in personal and social conduct and to know the real nature of man through practice of spirituality. Self-improvement involves control of thoughts and passions, silencing feelings, and removing complexes. In short, the quest is about changing human nature and human consciousness towards divinity. The sages have provided several methods for spiritual development; some are more meritorious and more effective than others. Bur since each person is different and unique in a way, there can be no generalization of the method to be adopted. No one method can be labeled as the best. Moreover, there is no point in comparing one method with the other since each individual has his own special way. Each case is different because each person has a different heredity, temperament, character, environment and living habits. Therefore there are as many paths from man to God as there are men. People are different by intellectual development, emotional temperaments, moral capacities and intuitional sensitivity. They have different needs, circumstances, outlooks, and possibilities. The seekers are different in starting points, personalities, motives and allegiances. They are different in their outer circumstances and inner conditions, their historical background and geographical locality, their karmic destiny and evolutionary need. They are different in their competence too. The variety of methods developed is therefore is in conformity with the different needs of the seekers. There is thus no universally applicable prescription, except that the improvement in conduct and practice of meditation is a must. Even the techniques adopted for meditation are many. While the paths are many, the goal is the same'

'But what is the goal?' I asked, to which he replied, 'the ultimate goal is to discover that there is one reality, of which all are but a part, that the separateness of the personal ego is but superficial and that truth is evidenced by the consciousness of unity. It is to forget oneself but to remember the Atman. The result of this discovery is that the life is dedicated to the service of all creatures, a life of universal welfare. The goal of spirituality involves subduing personal ego under the Atman, giving the ego a secondary place to the primary place of the will of God. The result of this spiritual effort is to make one an enlightened and balanced human being. It is to have a controlled mind and a more virtuous life and to be aware of the divine self within. To achieve this, thoughts, feelings, will and intuition are used in a special way. It is a long and arduous exercise that requires a great personal discipline. Just because only a few succeed in this venture is no reason to skip this aspect of life. Whatever progress is made stays with the person and that itself is a great reward for the effort. '

THE DIVINE INTELLIGENCE

SPIRITUAL DEVELOPMENT

"Is the spiritual quest an endless adventure, never to become a final achievement?

Are its goals too high for a common man?"

"The fact that men have achieved the final goal provides optimism. If we feel the goal cannot be achieved in one life time, then do what you can in your life and leave the rest to be done in later lives"

"Is it necessary to travel far in the search for a master or a guru?"

"It is not necessary to travel far and wide. Search within, for the truth lies there. You only need to move from noise to silence and from external to inner world for meditation. Look deeper into your heart there lies what you seek. When you move to outer places, your ego moves with you. Enlightenment involves liberation from ego. You can do it at any place when you are able to meditate."

"What does the process of spiritual development involve?"

"The Upanishad states: *Shravan* (listening), *Manan* (reflection), *Samadhi* (deep meditation) *shravan* is receiving instructions through self-study or through a guru, *manan* is thinking over the studied texts till the instruction is assimilated, *samadhi* is to experience the mystical reality. The goal is the continuous experience of spiritual reality which is termed enlightenment, a state of wisdom and peace."

"How long it takes to complete spiritual development?"

" There is no fixed time. It is a lifelong process. Depending on circumstances, previous development and the effort put in, it may take lesser time. But it is rare to achieve in a few years though there are some cases of instant enlightenment."

"What are the signs of progress?"

"The momentary glimpse of the Atman, the reality, provides the real beginning and the uninterrupted realization is the final ending."

"What are the stages of development?"

"Step 1: belief in God is the prerequisite. Then gain knowledge. Withdraw senses from outside objects. Establish the belief that matter is not the ultimate reality.

Step 2: worship God in some form. Aspire for self-improvement by building character and conduct. Affirm spirit as the ultimate reality. Develop the witness attitude, detachment from world's activities, and the *vairagya bhava*.

Step 3: Acquire knowledge and experience of Atman, the inner reality

Step 4: Experience love of God expressed as love for all. See the unity with life in the world. Realize all in oneself and oneself in all. Do service of mankind as service to God. This is God-consciousness"

"What do you gain by following the spiritual path?"

"In following the spiritual path the first reward is that one's lower self, the body and the sense mind, becomes subservient to the soul. The second reward is the inner peace. Inwardly you become intensely satisfying and joyous. You find that heaven is not a place in space but a condition of being. A feeling of serenity fills the person.

As a result of the spiritual exercises, the person brings conflicting emotions to rest, trains his thoughts, wins over the ego and achieves a state of peace. He develops perfect equanimity between joy and sorrow. The inner peace and a virtuous conduct are easily perceptible. Intuition too becomes stronger and helps the person in the conduct of worldly affairs better. Right thinking makes him wiser. Calmness and intuition are the glaringly visible advantages of spiritualization.

It is the ego that makes mistakes and causes suffering. The Atman, or the inner reality, brings pure and uninterrupted joy, calmness and wisdom. Spiritualization makes one sensitive and sympathetic to the sufferings of others. A spiritual person becomes patient, stable, self controlled, peaceful, and even-minded and develops love for all as God does.

The rewards of spirituality are not material. They concern the mind more than the body. The biggest reward is that one comes closer to the *Atmic* consciousness. A spiritual person has more inner peace and less inner anxiety. He has amity in relationships and less enmity with others.

The three fold path of right conduct, self study of spiritual texts and practice of meditation brings peace, satisfaction and intuitive wisdom."

"Are there any pitfalls and risks involved in this pursuit of spirituality?"

"Yes, there are. If the spiritual practices are improperly done, there may develop an indifference and disinterestedness in worldly duties. A casual approach may develop that affects one's every day practical life. One must not fall into the trap of seeking occult powers or psychic powers as an end objective. This may inflate the ego and push the person further into materialism. Psychic phenomena will excite the person while the true spiritual experience will calm the person and subdue the ego. Along with peace and joy the path has moments of gloom, difficulties, conflicts and vacillations. Any one suffering from mental disorders should first get cured before starting meditation; other wise the disorders may get accentuated. Meditation done too long without adequate supervision may generate problems for the seeker. Also, one must first prepare oneself for meditation by improving one's personal and social conduct. All spiritual texts emphasize the importance of preparatory steps for proper results. Proper preparation before starting, and adequate supervision in later stages, are important. Nothing is gained without any effort. It is a universal law that has to be respected."

"What are the issues involved in teacher student relationship in spiritual development?"

"First of all the teacher should be an enlightened person himself. That means he must have traversed the path that he shows to the student. In addition, he should be truthful and compassionate. The teacher's guidance should take one away from the guidance of the ego. The relationship of the teacher with the student is mental. It relates to the inner being more than the physical nearness. The teacher must be honorable, selfless, experienced and an expert guide.

A spiritual teacher provides conviction about the existence of soul to the student and shows him the direction to seek it. Prophets, sages, saints and mystics are reminders of our divine linkage. They quicken our spiritual development by giving a boost to our inner life. Therefore, in the matter of spiritual development it is far better to work under guidance than without it.

The need of a spiritual guide is no doubt an important one. The guru shows the way at critical junctures and provides grace to move smoothly in the path to perfection. While the need for guru is important, proper choice is also important. One must use one's discrimination faculty in the selection of spiritual path as well as the spiritual teacher. One must apply intelligence as well as intuition and common sense in making the proper decision. The eagerness to seek a guru should not mask the need to have the right person as the guru.

Sometimes in the absence of a personal teacher, the writings of enlightened persons can be quite effective. They describe their experiences for the benefit of the seekers. The writings may be in the form of scriptures, sayings, or texts that inspire the reader and show the direction to the uninitiated. These are especially important for the independent minded seekers. Those who lived in the past and left their experiences in the print word can be a source of inspiration for the later generations. Writings of the Greek philosophers, Buddhist masters and saints and mystics of medieval period are the source of such inspiration. Bhagwadgita too, has inspired millions over the centuries. I have personally benefited a lot from the writings of great masters like Aurobindo, Radhakrishnan, Ramakrishna, Vivekananda and the sages of olden times like Shankara and Kabir."

"What is the correct time to seek the spiritual teacher?"

"It is said, and is well known in spiritual circles, that when a pupil is ready, the master will appear. It means when the search for truth is most intense and the preparation is complete, the guru will appear to help the seeker. When we say that guru will appear at the right time, it only means that he will come into seeker's life in one way or the other. The mysterious forces prevailing at the time will arrange for the circumstances to bring the right person, or the right text or the inner voice at the right time into the life of the seeker to take him further. For this to happen, of course, the desire to seek guidance must be intense too. To know whether you have got the right person as your guru, you must inwardly feel an affinity with him even at the first meeting. Without this inner feeling, you may at times think that you have made a wrong judgment in accepting him as your guru. This one to one inner affinity is essential for smooth progress.

You must also agree with the philosophy that he preaches. Otherwise there will be doubts in your mind. The affinity with the guru is necessary to make a telepathic contact with him at times when you are away from him and need his guidance."

"Finding a spiritual guru is always a problem. How does one judge a good teacher from a not so good teacher?"

" A good spiritual teacher must be modest, serene and intuitive. A good teacher is judged from his mind and not from his personal appearance. One must use reason or intuition to judge a teacher. Our senses judge only the external parameters, which are of no concern in the choice of a good teacher. Spiritual help is given only to that person who is willing, worthy and ready to receive instruction. It should be given by that who is suitably qualified, properly equipped, and highly motivated. The spiritual teacher should be in communion with his higher self or fully united with it. He should restate the old truths in the modern context. He should not act as an intermediary with God but only as a counselor. He should feel himself to be an instrument of higher power and not as the source of power himself. He should have reached the goal to which he leads others. He should be a man of experience and not merely of intellectual insight. An honest spiritual guide should not make his disciples dependent on him but self-supporting in their pursuit. He should only instruct when a new direction is required to be shown to the seeker. He should make them guide themselves when the direction has been indicated. He must make them develop according to their personality and not be a mere copy of the teacher. A good teacher seeks anonymity and not publicity in his work. He should work for the day when his influence or interference is brought down to minimum. The good teacher should not point to his own importance but to the higher self of the disciple. He makes no material demands on his disciples and seeks no rewards for his effort. He seeks neither money nor personal power. He should not only communicate truth intellectually but also should live the truth in his life. He must set an example of ethical and moral life by his actions in the world and must have the experience of guiding different kinds of disciples.

It is not easy to know who is an enlightened master. But it is easy to know who is not. The seeker must judge from the personal conduct and public teaching of the person that he wants to adopt as his teacher. The enlightened person will have compassion, self-restraint, nonattachment, and calmness. A false one will indulge in malice, backbiting, greed, lust and anger. The good guru should be without personal ambition and greed and be liberated from the lower emotions. He does not bear any grudge nor becomes angry, if his advice is not heeded or ignored. A good guru must make distinction between spiritual teaching as a duty and spiritual teaching as a business. Spirituality is not a commodity to be bought or sold in a market place. A spiritually enlightened person may be perfect in spiritual matters but as a person he may not be perfect in all other matters. He may be inexperienced in certain matters and his opinion in such matters may not be of much value. The consciousness of an enlightened man may be perfect but in social conduct and scientific knowledge he may not be so. There is no faultless human. The enlightened man is also a human being and not God after all, though most of the time he is in communion with God. A wise person may not be wise all the time. The possibility of perfection in any person is debatable. The good teacher must point out the faults and weaknesses of the disciple and not pamper him. It may be the disciple's ignorance, ego or the prejudice. A good teacher is one who stimulates thought and does not impose it. He should not encourage a blind and unquestioning acceptance of his views. He may offer advice and suggestions, be strict and firm but not be dictatorial in issuing orders and dictating decisions. He should refrain from imposing his will and encourage natural growth of spirituality in the seeker. An ideal teacher helps his pupils to help themselves. He allows certain independence of thought as related to his spiritual development. A good teacher adapts his advice to fit each disciple individually. There are three things that a student expects from his spiritual teacher: development of philosophical intelligence, the practice of meditation and a virtuous existence".

"Just as there are do's and don'ts for a teacher there must be some for the students as well."

"Yes there are. The student should give all his devotion to the guru; treat him as an ideal but not an idol. He should keep his contact with the teacher through remembrance, devotion, faith and meditation. There should be complete confidence between student and teacher. There is a period of purification of character in which his animal nature and ego are minimized or removed and he is sensitized to intuition. Faith in the master is the first step. Obedience comes next, devotion is the third step and remembrance of teacher's presence is the fourth. These steps bring the grace of the guru. The student should be of good moral character and intelligent enough to follow the master's instructions. He should also be practical in approach, have mystical intuition and a sense of reverence. He should be dependable and reliable, should not be temperamental or liable to be easily disturbed. The first and foremost qualification of the student is the intense desire to know the truth. He should have the belief that God is working through the medium of the guru. He must be patient enough to wait for the results of his effort. He must possess the desired humility, reverence, obedience and loyalty. He must not be egoistic and self-opinionated. The disciple should make efforts to develop a high moral character together with religious aspiration and mystical contemplation as preparation for being a good student. Spiritual awareness cannot be transferred from one to another. It must come through hard work by the seeker. One must not become over dependent on the teacher. The student needs the quality of self-reliance in good measure. Where inner affinity exists between the spiritual teacher and the student, the spiritual guide can project calming, uplifting and spiritualizing mental waves to the aspirant. Unlike teaching in conventional mediums of instruction, the spiritual teaching can also be affected in silence since it is a communication through telepathic connection existing between the teacher and the student. The student needs to be receptive in mental tuning with the teacher."

"Who is the real teacher, the Atman or the physical being of the guru?"

"The teacher must be seen in the unity of the Atman of the student and that of the teacher. In a sense, it is the Atman that is the true guide. The teacher's voice is the voice of one's own Atman, the conscience that guides every one. When you appeal to the spiritual teacher or God, you are in fact appealing to your own inner being. The master is seen as the symbol of universal consciousness, the supreme Atman. He is a human symbol of the Infinite. The spiritual teacher or God or any other external symbol of your inner being is the one that guides you in your spiritual path. When this realization dawns, the guru becomes redundant."

THE MULTILEVEL BEING - LEVELS OF EXISTENCE

It was a cold and dark night, a moonless night where only the distant stars sent the dim light to make their presence felt. The cold wave sent shivers down the spine to the unprotected body. I was at the prayer meeting at a friend's place and shared the solemnity of the occasion with another friend. A priest was reciting portions of a sacred book and advising the audience to take the path of righteousness and wisdom. In this environment, people generally think of the purpose of life and talk of the need to do good in order to avoid the wrath of God.

In tune with the atmosphere prevailing, I asked my friend, ' is it true that God resides in the seventh or the fifth heaven as the scriptures of some religions state? Is it a physical reality or a mere symbolism of the state of mind that we attain by spiritual effort?' My friend did not answer, as he did not want to disturb the ambience of the occasion. He said he would satisfy my curiosity later.

On our return from the meeting, I repeated my query and he said, ' there is a religious belief among many people that God resides in the seventh or the fifth level from our level of existence. In the Upanishad, the Panchkoshi concept defines this level as the fifth while in general belief people say that God resides in the seventh heaven. However, the exact number is not important. What is important is the belief that the Reality is shrouded in multilevel existence; that the divine level and the human level of mundane existence are separated by certain levels of increasing subtlety and decreasing grossness as we rise in consciousness. Some of these levels are marked by mental existence, a subtler existence than the gross existence in matter. These levels are of the intuitive state, the subtler levels of the spiritual states of universal consciousness and God consciousness. The starting level is that of bodily existence, the grossest form, while the last is of the subtlest form, the pure consciousness.

Parallel to this thinking, there is a scientific assertion that reality is of higher dimension than the material existence. Reality is supposed to be of the 9th or the 10th dimension compared to our 4-dimensional existence. If we consider each level of higher existence as a separate level, then the four-dimensional gross existence will rise to the 9th level of subtlety as we reach the ultimate level of existence. We term this ultimate level as the level of Godly existence or the Reality. This is an interesting coincidence between the spiritual existence of God and the scientific reality of the ultimate level of existence. . Each subtler level raises the existence to a higher dimension and is more powerful in spiritual terms. The ninth dimensional Reality is thus the level of God's existence, the one we call as the ultimate reality. The grossest existence is the matter in space-time domain while the highest level is the nine dimensional reality of subtlest existence we designate as the pure blissful consciousness, or the God of religion.'

This association of the levels of spiritual existence and the higher dimensional life set me thinking of the unity in different approaches to the same reality.

SYMBOLIC REPRESENTATION OF SUPREME POWER

I do not know whether you have experienced the state of mind when you are not thinking of anything specific but random thoughts float around as vagrant clouds. I was in this frame of mind when a thought struck me. It was the significance of symbolism in our daily religious rituals that we take for granted but never care to understand.

External aspects of religion such as going to the place of worship, lighting lamp or candle and ringing bells have deeper meaning than we ever care to appreciate. The light and sound are symbols of the great power that we know as God. Knowledge (light) and the word (sound) are symbolic of the supreme power, the creative force that lies embedded in all creation. We go to the temple or mosque to meditate on that Power that rules our life. We seek strength from it in our body and mind. We seek a part of that infinite power in our being in order to face the difficulties in our daily life. By appealing to that power, we in fact appeal to our subconscious wherein lies a part of that power. We surrender to that power, knowing the immense extent of that power, a power that creates and sustains its creation. We even symbolize that power in our spiritual teacher or any other object that we like or worship. If we ignore the symbolism and take literally the form as the ultimate power, we give space to superstition. If we perform rituals without understanding the symbolism, we invite superstition in our life. There is no harm in worshipping a stone as God provided we understand that the stone is the symbol of the great power that has created the whole universe including us, and that power is as much present in the stone as within us.

Symbolism is deep rooted in most religions. The moment we discard symbolism and take things literally, we invite superstition in religion. Idol worship is criticized because symbolism of an idol is ignored and the idol is taken literally for something that it is not. In matters of symbolism, a spiritual guru is as good as an idol because both represent the same supreme power in material form that attracts reverence and worship.

Mythological tales are also full of symbolism. The power assigned to gods is the power of ultimate reality that empowers every body. Light and sound are symbolic of the creative energy. Shiva and Shakti are symbolic of the pure consciousness and the creative energy, which together constitute the conscious energy present in all creation.

Religious festivals too have a lot of symbolic significance. Burning fires, offering items of daily use to the fire god and taking *prasad* are symbolic of paying our respects to the supreme power and receiving its grace in return. Community singing and rejoicing offers an occasion for finding unity among the souls that are part of the same supreme power.

Symbolism in religious matters is not a convenience or a luxury but a necessity. The nature of God being infinite, eternal and mysterious, it is necessary to symbolize it by an entity, which may be a word, an object or a thing that we can relate to. An abstraction for visualization by necessity has to be a thing that our senses can relate to. A point of light, a geometrical figure, a word or a sentence, an image or a sculpture has all been used for this symbolization. It is a requirement for the mind, a thing or an object on which it can concentrate to avoid distraction.

The reality that is being symbolized is the feeling of just being, a feeling of pure joy and bliss. This cannot be described but can only be felt. No thing or object can truly represent it. That is why we have to symbolize it variously in order to relate to it. It is the knowledge of just being, the knowledge of joyous existence, the cause of all creation.

WHOM DO I PRAY?

Do I pray to an old man with a white beard?
Sitting in the seventh heaven and dispensing justice
Creating and playing with lives down below
And destroying at will

Do I pray to an abstraction, a void?
Symbolized by light, sound, Om or Swastika,
Believing that abstraction listens to my pleadings
And answers my prayer

Do I pray to an Invisible Presence?
That assures me, helps me and remains
Always in the background away from my eyes
The presence that I feel within me and without
By its effect on my surroundings

Do I pray only to myself?
My subconscious, my true nature,
My conscience, the light within
That is one with the Intelligence
That drives the world and the universe

I do not know for sure
But it does give me results
And that is what matters
And makes me grateful
To that Presence within and without

THE RELIGIOUS LIFE OF A SCIENTIST

On the face of it the title looks contradictory since there is a fundamental difference in the way a scientist looks at the world and a religious man sees the world. The scientist thinks that life is an accident of nature in which circumstances developed to evolve life. The religious man on the other hand thinks that intelligence is at the root of creation where everything in nature has evolved as per a grand design. Religiosity of a scientist is therefore a contradiction though many scientists are religious at heart. I personally think that it is not difficult or even strange for a scientist to be religious because he can keep his religiosity separate from his scientific pursuit. He may or may not believe in the Universal Intelligence that allows the creation to evolve in its myriad ways towards a highly developed conscious state, a state that a religious person would like to call as a divine state. His belief in this intelligence should not affect his scientific work since his work concerns about certain laws whose origin he is not worried about. He is not concerned about why the cosmic laws of gravity and electromagnetic forces exist. He is only concerned about how these laws operate and in turn run the cosmic events. The why part of investigation is in the realm of metaphysics where philosophic conjectures are involved.

However, from the simple hydrogen molecule to the most complex bio molecule, there is definite intelligence involved in evolution. The religious one may personify this intelligence as God but from the scientist's point of view it is a guiding force inherent in the structure. This intelligence works differently at different levels and is a multidimensional reality. We see it differently at different levels, sometimes matter and sometime pure energy. Its grossness differs at different levels till it becomes too subtle to visualize.

The scientist wonders at the vastness, complexity and variety in the universe. He wonders at the forces behind creation. He may not like to use words like God and divine for the universal intelligence but he is certainly concerned with the ultimate reality that transforms into this wonderful creation. His God may not be personified but he cannot but wonder how this whole universe has come about to its present state. He tries to solve the riddle of creation in his own way with the logic of mathematics and imagination of the poet. He frames philosophical propositions and tries to get evidence for his hypotheses. He devises experiments to test his theories, all in the search for truth. He does not want to speculate about God but he finds the same reality in every speck of matter. He too seeks the reality through the laws of universe and is eager to find the one unified force that runs the universe. That unified force is his God. When he discovers the intra-atomic and inter atomic forces at work, he cannot but wonder at the marvelous unity underlying the material creation. That is his devotional delight, a joyous wonder at the complexity of material creation that beckons one to explore further. The discovery of the unity behind material objects and living beings makes him develop a healthy respect for the intelligence in nature and a deep yearning for opening the secrets of the cosmic riddle. The tremendous energy, the explosive events of the cosmos and the fine balance of forces all make him wonder at the one reality that religions call God.

SCIENTIFIC OUTLOOK OF A RELIGIOUS PERSON

I have a belief that if a religious person had a

scientific temper he would be a much better religious person. If he watched the growth of plant and animal life, he would know the high level of intelligence involved in natural processes; how a seed takes shape of a plant, how the animal after birth learns to walk and feed itself and so on. The nature presents examples of its intelligence at every process of growth and sustenance. The regularity and precision of seasonal changes, the orbits of planets, the making of stars and the production of material elements in their cores are events of wonder that we find in nature where intelligence seems to work. For millions and billions of years the cosmic bodies keep their movement going in regular fashion, emitting radiation that travels trillions of miles. The precision of physical constants and the enormity of mass and radiation of big stars and galaxies, the presence of black holes and white dwarfs make us wonder at the ingenuity of universal existence. They all make us humble. We appreciate the intelligence and marvel at the cosmic forces that govern our lives and sustain the universe. Looking at the starry sky, who would not develop a respect for the enormity and complexity of nature. To call it a mere accidental happening would be trivializing the issue and a gross oversimplification. There has to be an intelligence of high order behind all this creation and sustenance of astronomical structure; the micro world of fundamental particles, the huge sources of radiation, the enormous energy in matter and antimatter, the large range of mass, length and frequencies encountered in universe and so on.

If the religious man develops an interest in astronomy, he would find himself a speck of sand in the great Sahara; he would find his personality, about which he is so proud, insignificant in the vastness of space. Even the earth, about which many warrior kings boasted of winning, is so small and insignificant in the vast universe. This realization will puncture the ego of the most boastful, and will chasten him to have respect for the great reality that runs the universe.

If he developed an interest in the particle physics, he would know that every material object is formed out of the same creative energy that manifests in the whole universe and is the reality of all creation. The unity with every living being at the fundamental level makes him see the futility of waging wars and the meaninglessness of the desire to dominate others. The realization of equality fills one with a sense of fraternity and one sees everywhere that infinite and eternal energy that is the source, the cause and the reality of every material object, living or non living.

If the person develops interest in genetics, he would find that 99.9% of genes of all persons are alike thereby telling us that we are all made of the same stuff. Hating others is therefore just being silly. Nature has made us all equal but our thoughts have made us different. We have moved away from nature, we divided into groups and subgroups, created boundaries and cocooned ourselves in various social structures. Nature does not distinguish between us. It provides its rewards and fruits equally. But we are ego ridden and take pride in our prejudices based on caste, creed, color or social standing.

Scientific knowledge therefore strengthens the religious belief of equality and brotherhood. The person is filled with a sense of humility before nature, the nature that is kind and benevolent to one and all. The pride of power and wealth melts away before the grandeur of nature. The person knows that he/she is nothing but a tiny part of that vast universal energy that is present everywhere.